RELIABILITY

J . PATRICK MEYER

RELIABILITY

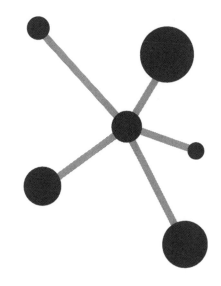

OXFORD
UNIVERSITY PRESS
2010

OXFORD
UNIVERSITY PRESS

Oxford University Press, Inc., publishes works that further Oxford University's
objective of excellence in research, scholarship, and education.

Oxford   New York
Auckland   Cape Town   Dar es Salaam   Hong Kong   Karachi
Kuala Lumpur   Madrid   Melbourne   Mexico City   Nairobi
New Delhi   Shanghai   Taipei   Toronto

With offices in
Argentina   Austria   Brazil   Chile   Czech Republic   France   Greece
Guatemala   Hungary   Italy   Japan   Poland   Portugal   Singapore
South Korea   Switzerland   Thailand   Turkey   Ukraine   Vietnam

Copyright © 2010 by Oxford University Press, Inc.

Published by Oxford University Press, Inc.
198 Madison Avenue, New York, New York 10016

www.oup.com

Oxford is a registered trademark of Oxford University Press, Inc.

Library of Congress Cataloging-in-Publication Data

Meyer, J. Patrick.
Reliability / J. Patrick Meyer.
p.   cm. — (Series in understanding statistics)
Includes bibliographical references.
ISBN 978-0-19-538036-1
1. Psychometrics.   2. Psychological tests—Evaluation.   3. Educational tests
and measurements—Evaluation.   4. Examinations—Scoring.   I. Title.
BF39.M487 2010
150.28'7—dc22
2009026618

9 8 7 6 5 4 3 2 1

Printed in the United States of America

In loving memory of my mother, Dottie Meyer

ACKNOWLEDGMENTS

I owe many thanks to my wife Christina and son Aidan for their loving support and encouragement. You were very patient with me as I spent many nights and weekends writing this manuscript. I love you both, and I am forever grateful for your support.

I would like to thank the South Carolina Department of Education for the use of the Benchmark Assessment and the Palmetto Achievement Challenge Test data. Special thanks are extended to Teri Siskind, Robin Rivers, Elizabeth Jones, Imelda Go, and Dawn Mazzie. I also thank Joe Saunders for his help with the PACT data files and Christy Schneider for discussing parts of the analysis with me.

I am very grateful for the help and support of colleagues at the University of Virginia. In particular, I thank Billie-Jo Grant for providing feedback on earlier drafts. Your input was invaluable and produced needed improvements to the manuscript. I also thank Sara Rimm-Kaufman and Temple Walkowiak for writing a description of the Responsive Classroom Efficacy Study and allowing me to use the MSCAN data.

CONTENTS

RELIABILITY

1

INTRODUCTION

Context and Overview

SOCIAL SCIENTISTS frequently measure unobservable characteristics of people such as mathematics achievement or musical aptitude. These unobservable characteristics are also referred to as *constructs* or *latent traits*. To accomplish this task, educational and psychological tests are designed to elicit observable behaviors that are hypothesized to be due to the underlying construct. For example, math achievement manifests in an examinee's ability to select the correct answer to mathematical questions, and a flautist's musical aptitude manifests in the ratings of a music performance task. Points are awarded for certain behaviors, and an examinee's *observed score* is the sum of these points. For example, each item on a 60-item multiple-choice test may be awarded 1 point for a correct response and 0 points for an incorrect response. An examinee's observed score is the sum of the points awarded. In this manner, a score is assigned to an observable behavior that is posited to be due to some underlying construct.

Simply eliciting a certain type of behavior is not sufficient for educational and psychological measurement. Rather, the scores ascribed to these behaviors should exhibit certain properties: the scores should be consistent and lead to the proper interpretation of the construct. The former property is a matter of test score reliability, whereas the latter concerns test score validation (Kane, 2006). Test score *reliability* refers to the degree of test score consistency over many replications of a test or performance task. It is inversely related to the concept of *measurement error*, which reflects the discrepancy of an examinee's scores over many replications. Reliability and measurement error are the focus of this text. The extent to which test scores lead to proper interpretation of the construct is a matter of test validity and is the subject of another volume in this series.

The Importance of Test Score Reliability

Spearman (1904) recognized that measuring unobservable characteristics, such as mathematics achievement or musical aptitude, is not as deterministic as measuring physical attributes, such as the length of someone's arm or leg. Indeed, he acknowledged that measurement error contributed to random variation among repeated measurements of the same unobservable entity. For example, an examinee may be distracted during one administration of a math test but not during another, causing a fluctuation in test scores. Similarly, a flautist may perform one set of excerpts better than another set, producing slight variations in the ratings of musical aptitude. These random variations are due to measurement error and are undesirable characteristics of scores from a test or performance assessment. Therefore, one task in measurement is to quantify the impact on observed test scores of one or more sources of measurement error. Understanding the impact of measurement error is important because it affects (a) statistics computed from observed scores, (b) decisions made about examinees, and (c) test score inferences.

Spearman (1904, 1910) showed that measurement error attenuates the correlation between two measures, but other statistics are affected as well (see Ree & Carretta, 2006). Test statistics, such as the independent samples t-test, involve observed score variance in their computation, and measurement error increases observed score variance. Consequently, measurement error causes test statistics and effect size to be smaller, confidence intervals to be wider, and statistical power to be lower than they should be (Kopriva & Shaw, 1991). For example, Cohen's *d* is the effect size for an experimental design suitable for a independent-samples t-test.

An effect size of $d = 0.67$ that is obtained when reliability is 1.0 notably decreases as reliability decreases; decreasing reliability to .8 attenuates the effect size to .60, and decreasing reliability to .5 attenuates effect size to .47. Figure 1.1 demonstrates the impact of this effect on statistical power for an independent-samples t-test. The horizontal line marks the statistical power of 0.8. The curved lines represent power as a function of sample size per group for score reliabilities of 1.0, 0.8, and 0.5. Notice that as reliability decreases, more examinees are needed per group to maintain a power of 0.8. Indeed, a dramatic difference exists between scores that are perfectly, but unrealistically, reliable and scores that are not reliable. Given the influence of reliability on statistics, the conclusions and inferences based on these statistics may be erroneous and misleading if scores are presumed to be perfectly reliable.

Although biased statistics are of concern, some of the greatest consequences of measurement error are found in applications that

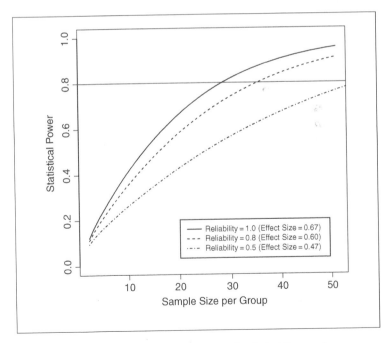

Figure 1.1. The Influence of Reliability on the Statistical Power of a Two-sample t-Test

concern the simple reporting of scores for individual examinees. Many uses of test scores involve high-stakes consequences for the examinee. For example, a student may be granted or denied graduation because of a score on a mathematics exam. An applicant may be granted or denied a job because of a score obtained on a measure of some characteristic desired by an employer. Because of such high stakes, test scores assigned to an examinee over many replications should be consistent. We cannot have confidence in test scores if the decision about an examinee (e.g., granted or denied graduation) differed from one administration of the test to another without any true change in the examinee's capability. Sizable measurement error can produce inconsistent decisions and reduce the quality of inferences based on those scores.

The amount of measurement error in test scores must be closely monitored, not only to appreciate the consistency of the test scores but also to evaluate the quality of the inferences based on the scores. Reliability is a "necessary but not sufficient condition for validity" (Linn & Gronlund, 2000, p. 108). Scores must be reliable in order to make valid inferences. If test scores are not consistent, there is no way to determine whether inferences based on those scores are accurate. Imagine watching someone throw darts at a dart board and trying to guess (i.e., infer) the score zone that the person is trying to hit. Suppose further that you have no knowledge of the thrower's intended target. If the darts hit the board in close proximity to each other, you have a good chance of correctly guessing the zone the person is trying to hit. Conversely, if the darts are widely dispersed, you have very little chance of correctly guessing the target score zone. Imagine that three darts are thrown and each hits a different score zone: What is the likely target? It could be any of the three zones or none of them. Wide dispersion of the darts would limit your confidence in guessing the intended target. Now suppose that all three darts hit close to each other in the 18 zone. What is the intended target? The 18 zone is a good guess for the intended target because of the consistency of their location.

Although reliability is a necessary condition for making valid inferences, it does not guarantee that our inferences about scores will be accurate. It is not a sufficient condition for validation. Scores may be reliably off-target. The tight grouping of darts described in the previous paragraph is indicative of reliability.

However, reliability does not guarantee that the darts are anywhere close to the target. Suppose you see three darts hit the bull's-eye but later learn that the thrower was aiming for the 20 zone! Your guess would have been a good one but nonetheless incorrect.

Reliability plays a key role in social science research and applied testing situations. It impacts the quality of test scores, statistical tests, and score inferences. Given the importance of reliability, the purpose of this book is to facilitate a thorough understanding of the selection, interpretation, and documentation of test score reliability.

Organization of the Book

Since Spearman's (1904) seminal work, various theories of test scores have evolved to address the technical challenges in the production of test scores and the characterization of score reliability. Classical test theory, classification decisions, and generalizability theory are three approaches discussed in this text. General concepts and commonalities among these theories are emphasized to make connections between them and facilitate an understanding of reliability. Distinctions between these theories are also discussed to appreciate the necessity of each theory and to help the psychometrician select an appropriate approach to characterizing score reliability.

Each book in the *Understanding Statistics* or *Understanding Measurement* series is organized around the same six chapters, as prescribed by the series editor. As a result, the development of concepts in this text differs from the development in other texts on reliability. Rather than have separate chapters for classical test theory, classification decisions, and generalizability theory, these approaches are discussed together and organized around a particular theme. For example, data collection designs for each theory are discussed in Chapter 2, whereas assumptions for each theory are described in Chapter 3. This structure presented some challenges in deciding how to best organize the material, and some readers may question my selection of content for each chapter. However, the organization of this text fits with modern data analysis and reporting techniques. Organizing the material in this manner will facilitate a deeper understanding of reliability as well as facilitate reliability analysis and reporting.

Chapter 1 presents an overview of classical test theory, classification decisions, strong true score theory, and generalizability theory. General concepts that cut across all topic areas are discussed, followed by a description of those concepts that are specific to each theory. Emphasis is placed on concepts that are central to understanding reliability and measurement error.

Chapter 2 begins with a description of data obtained from an operational testing program. This data will provide a basis for many of the explanations and examples throughout the text. It is followed by a description of data collection designs used in reliability analysis. An emphasis is placed on describing the type or types of measurement error present in each design.

Assumptions in classical test theory, classification decisions, and generalizability theory are described in Chapter 3. Particular attention is given to assumptions involving the nature of measurement procedure replications, and the consequences of these assumptions on the part-test covariance matrix.

Chapters 1 through 3 provide the theoretical basis for selecting a method of estimating reliability and reporting the results. Chapter 4 describes a variety of methods for estimating reliability. These methods are organized in decision trees to facilitate the selection of an appropriate method.

Reporting conventions described in Chapter 5 are based on guidelines set forth in the *Standards for Educational and Psychological Testing* (American Educational Research Association, American Psychological Association, & National Council on Measurement in Education, 1999). While it may seem unnecessary to discuss the reporting of reliability, several studies have shown that the literature is filled with poorly or improperly documented score reliability (Qualls & Moss, 1996; Thompson & Vacha-Haase, 2000; Vacha-Haase, Kogan, & Thompson, 2000). Guidelines for reporting reliability are illustrated with an analysis of scores from three different testing programs. Each program served a different purpose, which permitted a wide variety of reliability methods to be demonstrated. These examples are concluded in Chapter 6, with recommended strategies for discussing a reliability analysis.

Finally, this text is by no means exhaustive. Many others have written more technical and exhaustive works on one or more of the topics discussed herein. Chapter 6 also lists texts and other recommended readings in reliability.

General Concepts

Defining reliability as the degree of test score consistency conveys a general sense of what it means to be reliable—test scores should be consistent with something—but it lacks specification of the entities with which test scores should be consistent. A more complete definition of reliability would state something like, "Reliability is the extent to which test scores are consistent with another set of test scores produced from a similar process." Further improvements to this definition would state the specific details about the process that produced the test scores, such as information about the selection items for each test and the manner in which the data were collected. A general definition is useful in that it can apply to many situations; but in actuality, reliability is situation-specific. It only obtains its full meaning with a compete specification of the situation. For example, the statement, "Scores from a sixth grade math test are consistent," is incomplete. It does not indicate how the scores are consistent. The statement, "Scores from a sixth grade math test are consistent with scores obtained from the same examinees who took the same test but at a different time," is more complete and describes the process by which scores were obtained. It also differs from other possible statements such as, "Scores from a sixth grade math test are consistent with scores from a different but very similar sixth grade math test that was administered to the same examinees at a different time point." These two statements are more complete statements about score reliability, and they communicate very different notions of what it means for test scores to be consistent. Most importantly, they reflect different sources of measurement error. In the first statement, change in the examinee's state from one testing occasion to another is the primary source of error. The exact same test was used for each administration. Therefore, error due to lack of test similarity is not possible. In the second statement, scores may be inconsistent because of changes in an examinee's state from one administration of the test to another, as well as a lack of similarity between the two test forms. Although both of these statements refer to the extent to which sixth grade math test scores are consistent, the nature of the consistency and the sources of measurement error differ. Therefore, a complete understanding of the meaning of reliability is only possible through a complete specification of the process that produced the test scores.

The Measurement Procedure

When people think of educational and psychological measurement, they often think of individual tests. However, measurement involves much more than the test itself. The entire testing situation and the process that produces test scores must be considered. A *measurement procedure* (Lord & Novick, 1968, p. 302) encompasses all aspects of the testing situation, such as the occasion or time of test administration, the use of raters, the particular selection of test items, the mode of test administration, and the standardized conditions of testing (i.e., those aspects of testing that are fixed). It includes multiple aspects of the testing process, and it is not simply limited to the test itself. All aspects of the measurement procedure may affect the consistency of scores.

Sampling in Measurement

Sampling the Measurement Procedure. There are two types of sampling in measurement: the sampling of one or more aspects of the measurement procedure (e.g., items), and the sampling of examinees (see Cronbach & Shavelson, 2004; Lord, 1955b; Lord & Novick, 1968). The primary source or sources of measurement error are attributed to sampling the measurement procedure. For example, suppose a 50-item multiple-choice test of English language arts (ELA) is constructed from an item pool of 200 items, and this test is administered to a single examinee. Suppose further that any administration of this test occurs at the same time of day. The observed score that is obtained by counting the number of items answered correctly is only one of the 4.5386×10^{47} possible scores the examinee could earn from 50-item tests created from this pool of 200 items. It is very unlikely that the examinee will obtain the exact same score for all of these possible tests. Observed scores will vary due to the particular sample of items that comprise each test (i.e., measurement error due to the selection of items). One sample may be more difficult than another, or the examinee may be more familiar with some topics discussed in each item but not others. Other random aspects of the measurement procedure may also produce variation of observed scores. For example, the examinee may experience fatigue, distraction, or forgetfulness during the administration of some tests but not others.

Sampling the measurement procedure is also described as *replicating the measurement procedure* (Lord & Novick, 1968, p. 47). The latter phrase is preferred, given that the sampling may or may not involve simple random sampling. Avoiding use of the word "sampling" helps avoid the mistake of assuming that an instance of the measurement procedure was obtained through simple random sampling when it was not. Moreover, measurement procedure replications may involve samples with specific characteristics, such as prescribed relationships among observed score averages (see Chapter 3). The term "replication" helps convey the notion that the samples should have certain characteristics.

Brennan (2001a) stressed the importance of measurement procedure replications for the proper interpretation of reliability. He wrote that to understand reliability, "an investigator must have a clear answer to the following question: (1) What are the intended (possibly idealized) replications of the measurement procedure?" (p. 296). Continuing with the previous example, each sample of 50 ELA test items from the pool of 200 items may be considered a replication. Therefore, the consistency of scores that the examinee may obtain from all 50-item tests constructed from this pool reflects the similarity of test items. It does not reflect variation of scores due to testing occasion (e.g., testing in the morning rather than the afternoon) because each replication occurred at the same time of day. The meaning and interpretation of score reliability are inseparably tied to replicating the measurement procedure: "Reliability is a measure of the degree of consistency in examinee scores over replications of a measurement procedure" (Brennan, pp. 295–296). A clear definition of the measurement procedure and the process of replicating it provide a clear specification of the source or sources of error affecting scores and the interpretation of reliability.

As emphasized by Brennan, the replications may be idealized and only conceptual in nature. For example, the ELA item pool discussed previously may not actually exist. Rather, the item pool may be composed of all 50-item tests that *might be* created according to the test specifications. This type of conceptual replication is frequently encountered in practice. Even though there is no real item pool from which to sample items, only two real replications are necessary for estimating reliability, and these may be obtained by dividing a test into parts. All of the other possible replications do not need to occur, but they exist conceptually to facilitate the development of statistical theories underlying the scores and the interpretation of reliability.

Details of replicating the measurement procedure are particularly evident in the development of specific theories of test scores and the assumptions about test scores. Classical test theory, classification decisions, and generalizability theory define scores differently by imposing different restrictions on the way a measurement procedure is replicated. As a result, there are many different interpretations of reliability and methods for estimating it. For example, replications in classical test theory may use the administration of parallel test forms. In strong true score theory, replications may involve randomly sampling items from a domain. Generalizability theory permits the most exhaustive definition of a replication, such that multiple aspects of the measurement procedure may be considered simultaneously. For example, randomly sampling test forms and testing occasions may constitute a replication. As discussed in Chapter 3, the assumptions about test scores specify the nature of replicating the measurement procedure.

Sampling Examinees. Examinees participating in a measurement procedure are assumed to be randomly sampled from a population. If measurement error was held constant, and the population is heterogeneous on the construct of interest, then different scores would be observed for a group of examinees simply because of the process of randomly sampling examinees. For example, consider a population of examinees who differ in their mathematics ability. A random sample of two examinees would likely result in one examinee having better mathematical ability than the other. If error scores for these two examinees were the same, the observed score for the first examinee would be higher than the one for the second examinee. Therefore, variation among observed scores is due, in part, to randomly sampling examinees.

Replicating the Measurement Procedure and Sampling Examinees

Replicating the measurement procedure and sampling examinees do not occur in isolation. They occur in tandem. Every examinee in a sample has scores that are affected by sampling the measurement procedure. Therefore, the total variance of scores is made up of variance due to real differences among examinees and variance due to sampling the measurement procedure.

Table 1.1 contains an examinee-by-item matrix for the entire population and all conditions of the measurement procedure that are of possible interest. The observed score random variables are denoted by X, with subscripts that denote the row and column number, respectively. For example, X_{23} refers to the observed score random variable for the second person and the third item. In this example, the observed score random variable is the score on an individual item. Replicating the measurement procedure involves the selection of columns from the table, whereas sampling examinees involves the selection of rows from the table. Three possible samples of four examinees and two items are indicated by the shaded areas of Table 1.1. The total variability of observed scores in each shaded area will differ because of sampling items and examinees. Reliability coefficients provide an index that reflects the extent to which variation among real examinees differences (i.e., sampling rows) explains this total variability. However, reliability is a property of test scores from each sample. It is not a property of the test itself. Each sample will produce a different reliability estimate.

Table 1.1

The Infinite Matrix and Three Possible Samples of Four Examinees and Two Items

Examinee	Item								
	1	2	3	4	5	6	7	...	∞
1	X_{11}	X_{12}	X_{13}	X_{14}	X_{15}	X_{16}	X_{17}	...	$X_{1\infty}$
2	X_{21}	X_{22}	X_{23}	X_{24}	X_{25}	X_{26}	X_{27}	...	$X_{2\infty}$
3	X_{31}	X_{32}	X_{33}	X_{34}	X_{35}	X_{36}	X_{37}	...	$X_{3\infty}$
4	X_{41}	X_{42}	X_{43}	X_{44}	X_{45}	X_{46}	X_{47}	...	$X_{1\infty}$
5	X_{51}	X_{52}	X_{53}	X_{54}	X_{55}	X_{56}	X_{57}	...	$X_{5\infty}$
6	X_{61}	X_{62}	X_{63}	X_{64}	X_{65}	X_{66}	X_{67}	...	$X_{6\infty}$
7	X_{71}	X_{72}	X_{73}	X_{74}	X_{75}	X_{76}	X_{77}	...	$X_{7\infty}$
$\vdots$	$\vdots$	$\vdots$	$\vdots$	$\vdots$	$\vdots$	$\vdots$	$\vdots$	$\ddots$	$\vdots$
∞	$X_{\infty 1}$	$X_{\infty 2}$	$X_{\infty 3}$	$X_{\infty 4}$	$X_{\infty 5}$	$X_{\infty 6}$	$X_{\infty 7}$	...	$X_{\infty\infty}$

In the next three sections, important details and concepts in classical test theory, strong true score theory, and generalizability theory will be reviewed. This review is by no means exhaustive and the reader is encouraged to consult additional sources for a more technical and thorough review.

Classical Test Theory

Observed scores and error scores were previously defined in broad conceptual terms. However, they have a very specific definition in classical test theory. Moreover, they are related to a third type of score, the *true score*, which will be defined in more detail shortly. Observed scores, error scores, and true scores are related by a well-known formula,

$$X = T + E \tag{1.1}$$

where X, T, and E represent the observed, true, and error score for a randomly selected examinee, respectively.[1] The definitions of these scores are established with respect to replication of the measurement procedure.

Replicating the Measurement Procedure

An examinee's observed score is likely to differ upon each replication of the measurement procedure due to transient, internal characteristics of an examinee, such as forgetfulness, guessing, hunger, and distractibility. Variation among specific instances of the measurement procedure, such as using a different test form for each replication, also causes scores to vary from one replication to the next. Supposing that many (preferably infinite) replications of the measurement procedure have occurred, then an examinee will have many observed scores that vary randomly. A histogram could be used to graphically depict an examinee's observed score distribution, as illustrated in Figure 1.2. The top portion of this figure

---

[1] The letter T is actually the upper case Greek letter tau.

shows the distribution of observed scores obtained by an examinee over all possible replications of the measurement procedure. This distribution provides information about the amount of variability among observed scores, referred to as *examinee-specific observed score variance*, and the location of the distribution, referred to as the *true score*, which is marked by a thick solid vertical line in the bottom panel of Figure 1.2.

An examinee's true score is the score of primary interest in measurement. It is defined as an examinee's average observed score obtained from all replications of the measurement procedure. If an examinee actually participated in an infinite number of replications, we could compute the average observed score to obtain the actual true score. However, an examinee usually only participates in one or two replications of the measurement procedure, which is far short of the infinite number of replications

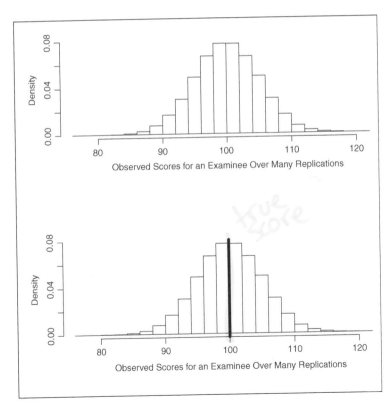

Figure 1.2. Observed Score Distribution for a Single Examinee

needed to obtain the actual true score. We never know the actual value of the true score, and we must estimate it from the observed scores that are actually obtained. While defining true scores in terms of an infinite number of observed scores appears as a limitation, this definition facilitates the statistical development of the theory and leads to methods for estimating the true score. It also results in a definition of the reliability coefficient, an index that describes the similarity of true and observed scores. Each of these methods will be discussed in detail later. Finally, this definition of a true score makes evident that a true score is not defined as some inherent aspect of the individual examinee. It is not something possessed, like hair color or weight. It is an abstraction defined in terms of replicating the measurement procedure.

Now that observed scores and true scores have been defined, the formal definition of error scores should be evident. The error score is simply the difference between an examinee's observed score and true score. Like an observed score, an examinee has a different error score for each replication of the measurement procedure, and all of these scores make up an error score distribution. This distribution has an average value of zero, but it has the same variance as the examinee's observed score distribution. Both of these characteristics are evident in Figure 1.3. Examinee-specific observed scores are displayed in the top panel of the figure, and examinee-specific error scores are depicted in the bottom panel. Notice the similarity of the two distributions. They have the same variance. Only the average value is different, as evident in the value of the bold vertical line. The observed score distribution has an average equal to the true score, whereas the error score distribution has an average value of zero.

In each replication of the measurement procedure, the goal is to obtain an observed score that is very close to an examinee's true score. When each replication of the measurement results in a small error score, the variance of the examinee-specific error score distribution will be small, and we can have confidence that our observed score is close to the true score on any one replication of the measurement procedure. Conversely, when each replication of the measurement procedure results in a large error score, the variance of the examinee-specific error score distribution will be large and indicate a large difference between observed scores and true score. A large variance of the examinee-specific error score

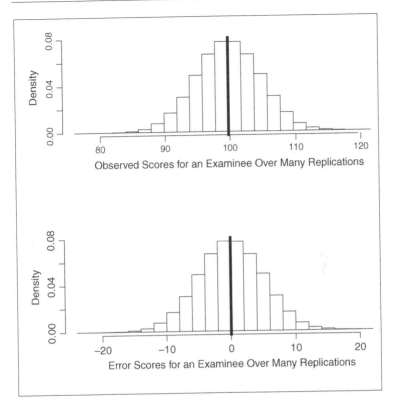

Figure 1.3. Examinee Specific Observed and Error Score Distributions

distribution means that our measurement procedure produced a lot of random noise. Our confidence in the quality of observed scores decreases as measurement error increases. However, measurement error to this point has been defined in terms of a single examinee who participates in many replications of the measurement procedure—a situation that rarely, if ever, holds in practice. Therefore, measurement error and reliability are defined with respect to a sample of examinees.

Additional Restrictions That Define Classical Test Theory. Several restrictions on the measurement procedure must be stated to complete the definition of classical test theory. The restrictions are that (a) the expected value (i.e., mean) of the examinee-specific error score distribution is zero, (b) there is no relationship between true scores and error scores, (c) there is no relationship between the error scores obtained from any two replications of the measurement procedure, and (d) there is no relationship between error scores obtained from one replication of the measurement procedure and true scores obtained from any other replication of the measurement procedure. The complete definition leads to important results in classical test theory, such as the decomposition of observed score variance and the development of reliability coefficient estimates.

Sources of Variance

The variance of observed scores over a sample of examinees is true score variance plus error score variance,

$$\sigma^2(X) = \sigma^2(T) + \sigma^2(E). \qquad (1.2)$$

The covariance between true and error scores is not part of this result, given restriction (b) listed in the previous paragraph. Observed score variance is the easiest term to explain. It is simply the variance of the scores obtained from every examinee in the sample.

True score variance is also easy to explain. The true score is fixed for a single examinee, and it is the same in all replications of the measurement procedure. There is no true score variance within an examinee. However, true scores vary for a sample of examinees. That is, each examinee likely will have a different true score. If each examinee's true score were known, we could compute the variance of the true scores for a sample of examinees to obtain the true score variance, $\sigma^2(T)$. However, each examinee's true score is unknown. True score variance must be estimated from observed score variance using certain methods that follow from classical test theory. These methods will be described later.

Error score variance is more difficult to define because error scores differ within an examinee (i.e., over replications), and each examinee has a different error variance. This aspect is illustrated in Figure 1.4 for three examinees, each with a different true score. Error score variance, $\sigma^2(E)$, for a sample of examinees is defined as the average (i.e., expected value) of the examinee-specific error

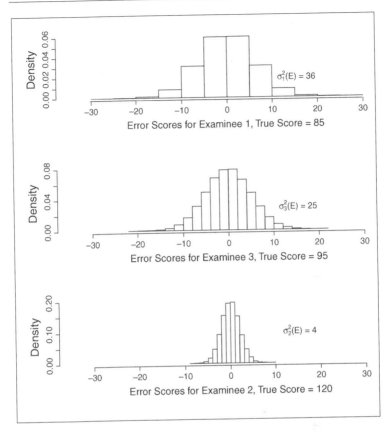

Figure 1.4. Error Score Distributions for Three Examinees

variances. If every examinee has a large examinee-specific error variance, then the average (over examinees) error variance will also be large. Conversely, if every examinee has a small examinee-specific error variance, then the average (over examinees) error variance will be small. For Figure 1.4, error variance is computed as $(25 + 4 + 36)/3 = 21.67$.

A difficulty in using a variance term to describe error is that it involves squared units. Therefore, the *standard error of measurement* is the square root of the average[2] of the examinee-specific

---

[2] More accurately, it is the expected value of the examinee-specific error variances. The term *average* is used for simplicity.

error variances. It describes the amount of measurement error using the same units (i.e., the same scale) as the test itself, rather than squared units. For the information in Figure 1.4, the standard error of measurement is $\sqrt{21.67} = 4.66$. In practice, error variance and the standard error of measurement is not so easy to compute because we do not know the true or error scores. Error score variance may also be estimated with certain methods, as described later.

Although using a statistic like the standard error of measurement that employs the same scale as the test is useful for interpretation, it limits comparisons among similar tests that use different scales. For example, suppose there are two tests of eighth grade ELAs that are proportionally built to the same specifications, but each test has a different number of items. If one test contains 60 items and another contains 90 items, and the observed score is the reporting metric, the tests have two different scales and the standard error of measurement may not be used to compare the quality of the two measures. A "scale-free" index is necessary to compare measures that involve different scales.

The Reliability Coefficient

Reliability is defined as the squared correlation between observed scores and true scores, and this index turns out to be the ratio of true score variance to observed score variance,

$$\rho_{XT}^2 = \frac{\sigma^2(T)}{\sigma^2(T) + \sigma^2(E)}. \tag{1.3}$$

Unlike the standard error of measurement, the reliability coefficient is scale-independent, and it may be used to compare the quality of measurement procedures that use different scales. The downside is that the reliability coefficient does not tell us how far observed scores deviate from true scores in the original metric. Therefore, a useful practice is reporting reliability and the standard error of measurement.

Traub and Rowley (1991, p. 175) provide a succinct explanation of the reliability coefficient and the meaning of its metric:

- It is a dimensionless number (i.e., it has no units).
- The maximum value of the reliability coefficient is 1, when all the variance of observed scores is attributable to true scores.
- The minimum value of the coefficient is 0, when there is no true-score variance and all the variance of observed scores is attributable to errors of measurement.
- In practice, any test that we may use will yield scores for which the reliability coefficient is between 0 and 1; the greater the reliability of the scores, the closer to 1 the associated reliability coefficient will be.

The fact that all reliability coefficients behave in the manner described by Traub and Rowley may perpetuate the myth that a test has only one reliability coefficient. For many people, a description of the reliability coefficient metric is the sole framework for interpreting reliability. However, as Brennan (2001a) points out, the interpretation of reliability is founded upon the notion of replicating the measurement procedure. This distinction is important. All estimates of the reliability coefficient will behave as described by Traub and Rowley, but each coefficient is interpreted differently depending upon the manner in which the measurement procedure is replicated.

Estimating Unobserved Quantities

Kelley (1947) provided a formula for estimating an examinee's true score. It is an empirical Bayes estimator that is computed as a weighted sum of an examinee's score, x, and the group average, μ_X, where the weight is an estimate of the reliability coefficient. Specifically, Kelley's equation, is given by

$$\hat{T} = \hat{\rho}_{XT}^2 x + (1 - \hat{\rho}_{XT}^2)\hat{\mu}_X. \qquad (1.4)$$

When reliability equals 1, the estimated true score is the examinee's observed score. If reliability equals 0, the estimated true score is the group average observed score. Kelley's equation is useful for reporting scores for examinees. All that is needed to obtain an estimated true score is an examinee's observed score, an estimate of the group average observed score, and an estimate of reliability.

True score variance and error variance may be defined in terms of observable quantities: observed score variance and reliability. Rearranging the definition of the reliability coefficient (Equation 1.3) results in an expression for the true score variance, $\sigma_T^2 = \sigma_X^2 \rho_{XT}^2$. True score variance may be estimated by substituting an estimate of observed score variance for σ_X^2 and an estimate of reliability for ρ_{XT}^2.

Error variance may also be expressed in terms of observable quantities by rearranging Equation 1.3, $\sigma_E^2 = \sigma_X^2(1 - \rho_{XT}^2)$. The square root of this value is the standard error of measurement (SEM), which is given by

$$SEM = \sigma_X \sqrt{1 - \rho_{XT}^2}. \qquad (1.5)$$

Error variance and the SEM may also be estimated by substituting an estimate of observed score variance (or standard deviation) and reliability into the preceding equations.

A $(\gamma \times 100)\%$ confidence interval for true scores is $X \pm z SEM$, where z is the $1 - (1 - \gamma)/2$ quantile from the standard normal distribution. This interval assumes that true scores have a unit normal distribution. A 95% confidence interval is obtained when $z = 1.96$.

This section defined classical test theory and presented some of the results of this definition, such as the decomposition of observed score variance and an expression for the reliability coefficient. To select an appropriate estimate of reliability and properly interpret it, the data collection design and underlying assumptions must be specified. Data collection designs will be discussed in the next chapter, along with implications for the proper interpretation of reliability. Chapter 3 will discuss different assumptions in classical test theory and explain how each further restricts the measurement procedure replications.

Classification Decisions

Test scores as numbers alone are meaningless. They must go through a process of scaling in order to take on meaning and have an interpretive frame of reference. Two common methods of providing a frame of reference for test scores are the creation of test norms and the establishment of cut-scores. *Test norms* reflect the distribution of scores for a given population, and they allow for the computation of auxiliary scores (Kolen, 2006), such as percentiles, which facilitate the interpretation of scores. A *percentile score* refers to the proportion of examinees that score at or below a particular level. For example, a score of 85 on a mathematics test says little about examinee achievement. If the norms indicate that a score of 85 falls in the 75th percentile, then we know that 75% of examinees obtained a score at or below 85. Moreover, this number is well above the median score and suggests an excellent level of mathematics achievement. The number 85 takes on much more meaning when reported in the context of test norms. Score interpretations in this situation are relative to other examinees, and a test used for this purpose is referred to as a *norm-referenced test* (Glaser, 1963).

Reporting test scores in a relative manner using percentiles or some other score based on norms does not always serve the purpose of testing. In many applications, such as licensure exams and high-stakes achievement tests, the purpose of testing is to determine where an examinee's score falls with respect to an absolute standard. A *cut-score* defines the boundary between two achievement levels, such as pass or fail, and this absolute standard is commonly established through a process of standard setting (see Cizek & Bunch, 2007). Licensure exams may have a single cut-score that defines the boundary between granting the license or not. Educational tests often have multiple achievement levels differentiated by multiple cut-scores. For example, the National Assessment of Educational Progress uses two cut-scores to define three achievement levels: Basic, Proficient, and Advanced (Allen, Carlson, & Zelenak, 1999, p. 251). Score interpretations in this setting are relative to the criterion (i.e., cut-score) and not other examinees. Tests that use cut-scores to distinguish different achievement levels are referred to as *criterion-referenced tests* (Glaser, 1963).

Norm-referenced and criterion-referenced tests differ not only in their implications for score interpretation, but also in their meaning of score reliability (Popham & Husek, 1969). Norm-referenced tests are design to spread out examinees to facilitate their rank ordering (i.e., relative comparison). As such, heterogeneity of true scores is desirable and will increase the classical test theory reliability coefficient. Criterion-referenced tests, on the other hand, are designed to classify examinees into achievement levels, and it is perfectly acceptable for all examinees to be placed in the same achievement level and have the same true score. As a result, the classical test theory reliability coefficient may be 0 even when all examinees are placed in the correct achievement level. Popham and Husek noted this distinction and indicated that reliability coefficients for norm-referenced tests are not appropriate for criterion-referenced tests.

Reliability for a criterion-referenced test must take into account the cut-score or cut-scores and evaluate the consistency of classifying examinees into achievement levels. One approach for defining a reliability coefficient for criterion-referenced tests involves the *squared error loss* (see Livingston, 1972). This method is based on classical test theory, and it adjusts the classical test theory reliability coefficient to take into account the distance between the average score and the cut-score. Brennan and Kane (1977) extended this approach to generalizability theory, as will be discussed in that section. The supposition in squared error loss methods is that achievement-level classification will be more correct when the average score is far away from the cut-score. However, this method does not quantify the consistency or accuracy of classifying examinees into the achievement levels. Hambleton and Novick (1973) make an argument for a second approach, *threshold loss*, that specifically evaluates whether an examinee's score is above or below a cut-score.

The foundation for squared error methods are covered in the sections on classical test theory and generalizability theory. Foundational concepts for threshold loss methods are provided in detail below, given that they differ from those discussed in classical test theory and generalizability theory.

Replicating the Measurement Procedure

Reliability methods for criterion-referenced tests make use of the notion of a domain score. A *domain* represents all of the items or tasks (either real or imagined) that correspond to the content area or construct of interest. It is more than just the items on a test or items that have actually been produced. It is a larger entity that represents all possible items that are considered appropriate for a measurement procedure. A domain is a *sampling frame* that defines the characteristics of the items that may be included in a measurement procedure. For example, the domain may be a bank of 10,000 items or all possible items that could be automatically generated by a computer (see Bejar, 1991).

A *domain score* is the proportion of items in the domain that an examinee can answer correctly (Crocker & Algina, 1986, p. 193). It is akin to a true score in classical test theory. Like a true score, the definition of a domain score involves many more replications of the measurement procedure than those that actually take place. Take a common statistics analogy for an example. Suppose an urn is filled with 100 white balls and 300 red balls. The true proportion of red balls is 0.75. Rather than count every ball in the urn, this proportion can be estimated by taking a random sample of, say, 30 balls. The proportion of balls in this sample of 30 is an estimate of the true proportion of balls in the urn. To make a more direct connection to testing, the domain is the urn of red and white balls. A red ball represents a correctly answered item, and a white ball represents an incorrectly answered item. Each examinee has a different number of red balls in the urn. An examinee's domain score is the true proportion of red balls in the urn (i.e., proportion of correctly answered items), and the observed score is the number of red balls in the sample of 30. Because of the simple act of sampling items from the domain, an examinee's observed score will differ from the domain score. Some random samples may involve higher estimates due to the inclusion of more items that can be answered correctly in the sample than those that can be answered incorrectly. Other random samples may result in lower estimates because the sample involves more items that can be answered incorrectly than those that can be answered correctly. The different estimates in this case are due to randomly sampling items from the domain.

Observed scores will vary due to randomly sampling items from the domain. Consequently, the proportion of examinees above and below the cut-score will also vary from one replication to another. *Decision consistency* refers to the extent to which

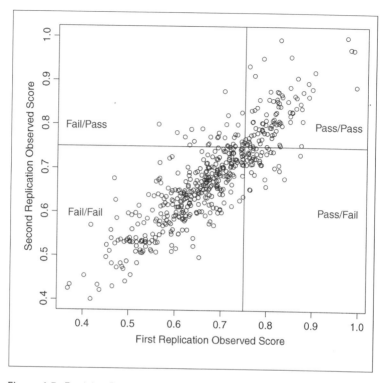

Figure 1.5. Decision Consistency for Two Replications and a Cut-score of 0.75

examinees are placed into the same achievement level on two replications of the measurement procedure. It is also referred to as *raw agreement* or the proportion of agreement. Figure 1.5 illustrates decision consistency for a sample of 500 examinees. The vertical and horizontal lines intersecting the plot identify the cut-score. Examinees placed in the upper-right and lower-left quadrant represent consistent decisions. The other two quadrants represent inconsistent decisions. Decision consistency is based on observed scores. Therefore, it is often of interest to also know the extent to which observed score classifications match true score classifications.

Decision accuracy refers the extent that achievement-level classification on the basis of observed scores agrees with classification based on domain (i.e., true) scores. Figure 1.6 illustrates decision accuracy for the same data illustrated in Figure 1.4 using observed scores from the first replication. Notice that the y-axis now refers

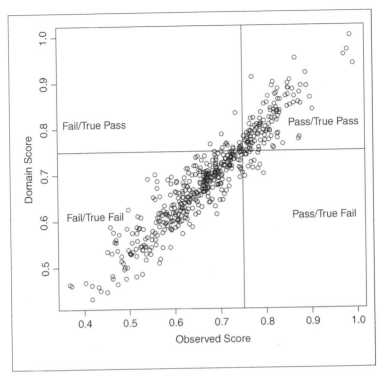

Figure 1.6. Decision Accuracy for a Cut-score of 0.75 (Note: $\rho^2_{XT} = 0.88$)

to domain scores, and the upper-right and lower-left quadrants represent instances when examinees are classified by domain scores in the same way that they are classified using observed scores.

Approaches for estimating decision consistency and decision accuracy require that a continuous score be divided into two or more discrete categories. For example, a score of 85 is transformed to a score of Basic, Proficient, or Advanced depending on the location of the cut-scores. Estimates are then based on these categorical variables.

Methods for estimating decision consistency and decision accuracy from two replications are relatively straight forward and simply quantify the information graphically summarized in Figures 1.5 and 1.6. When only one replication is involved, the methods become noticeably more complicated and require strong assumptions about the nature of true and observed scores. *Strong true score theory* refers to methods that make strong assumptions about the nature of test scores. These methods are considerably more complicated than those used in classical test theory or generalizability theory.

Strong true score theory will be introduced in the next section. Any presentation of this material is complicated, but an attempt is made to here describe it in as simple a manner as possible without completely omitting it.

Strong True Score Theory

Classical test theory assumes that test scores are continuous. It also stipulates certain relationships among the moments (e.g., mean and standard deviation) of the score distributions, although no particular distributions are specified. That is, the scores are not presumed to follow any specific probability distribution. Classical test theory is a distribution-free theory. Strong true score theory, on the other hand, does assume that scores follow a particular distribution. These additional assumptions are what gives rise to the "strong" in strong true score theory. The advantage of strong true score theory is that scores may be modeled with probability distributions, and the fit of the model can be evaluated. However, the disadvantage is that stronger assumptions are made about the scores and, if these assumptions are not appropriate, the model is of limited utility.

Distributional Assumptions

Domain Scores. The two-parameter beta distribution provides the probability of a domain score, θ, which ranges from 0 to 1. It has two shape parameters, α and β, and it is given by

$$f(\theta) = B(\alpha, \beta)\theta^{\alpha-1}(1 - \theta)^{\beta-1}, \tag{1.6}$$

where $B(\alpha, \beta)$ denotes the beta function. One would not compute Equation 1.6 by hand. It would only be computed using a computer.

Lord (1965) introduced a four-parameter beta distribution that restricts the lower (l) and upper (u) limits of the beta distribution, such that $0 \leq l \leq \theta \leq u \leq 1$. It is given by

$$f(\theta) = \frac{(-l + \theta)^{\alpha - 1}(u - \theta)^{\beta - 1}}{(u - 1)^{\alpha + \beta - 1}B(\alpha, \beta)}. \tag{1.7}$$

A benefit of these restrictions is that the lowest true scores may be restricted to account for random guessing. That is, domain scores lower than expected from random guessing have a 0 probability. Overall model fit, therefore, tends to be better with the four-parameter beta distribution.

Conditional Distribution of Observed Scores. Once a domain score is known, the binomial distribution provides the probability of an observed score for an n-item test. Specifically,

$$f(x|\theta) = \binom{n}{x}\theta^x + (1 - \theta)^{n - x}. \tag{1.8}$$

Unlike classical test theory, error scores in this model are not independent of domain scores. This feature results in a method for computing a conditional error variance, as described below. The challenge in computing this probability is that the examinee's domain score is unknown. However, it may be modeled with a probability distribution or estimated directly from the data, as described below.

Observed Scores. Keats and Lord (1962) demonstrated that when the conditional distribution of observed scores given domain scores is binomial, and the distribution of domain scores is a two-parameter beta distribution, the marginal distribution of observed scores follows a beta-binomial distribution,

$$h(x) = \binom{n}{x}\frac{B(x + \alpha, n - x + \beta)}{B(\alpha, \beta)}. \tag{1.9}$$

Furthermore, the two parameters are given by,

$$\alpha = \left(-1 + \frac{1}{r_{21}}\right)\hat{\mu}_X \qquad (1.10)$$

and,

$$\beta = -\alpha + \frac{n}{r_{21}} - n. \qquad (1.11)$$

Equation 1.9 provides the probability of a particular observed score, x, given the number of test items and estimates of the mean observed score, $\hat{\mu}_X$, and the Kuder-Richardson formula 21 reliability coefficient, r_{21}, (Kuder & Richardson, 1937). Unfortunately, Equation 1.9 is too complicated to compute by hand and must be evaluated with a computer. However, the advantage of Equation 1.9 is that it provides a way of modeling observed scores without regard for domain scores, and it lends itself to other applications in measurement, such as smoothing scores for equipercentile equating, as well as the derivation of decision consistency indices.

Lord (1965) combined the four-parameter beta distribution with the binomial distribution to compute a different form of Equation 1.9. His four-parameter beta-binomial distribution is not shown here, but it too will be denoted $h(x)$.

Estimating Domain Scores. If no distributional assumptions are made, an examinee's domain score may be estimated directly from the data using the maximum likelihood estimator, $\hat{\theta} = 1/n \sum_{i=1}^{n} x_i$, which is the proportion of items an examinee answers correctly. An empirical Bayes estimator is also possible under the condition that the examinee is from a group with a unimodal score distribution with group mean, $\hat{\mu}_X$. This estimator of the domain score is

$$\hat{\theta}^* = r_{21}\hat{\theta} + (1 - r_{21})\left(\frac{\hat{\mu}_X}{n}\right). \qquad (1.12)$$

This formula is Kelley's equation based on domain scores. If a measure has an r_{21} estimate of 1, then the maximum likelihood and empirical Bayes estimators are the same.

If domain scores are assumed to follow a two- or four-parameter beta distribution, the posterior distribution of domain scores given observed scores may be computed using Bayes theorem (see Hogg & Tanis, 2001) as

$$f(\theta|x) = \frac{f(x|\theta)f(\theta)}{h(x)}. \tag{1.13}$$

In this way, domain score estimates and 95% credible intervals for domain scores may be computed.

Alternatively, a $(\gamma \times 100)\%$ confidence interval for true scores may be obtained from the binomial error model by solving Equation 1.8 for the lower and upper bound. Clopper and Pearson (1934) define the lower, θ_L, and upper, θ_U, bounds of the confidence interval as

$$\sum_{i=X}^{n} \binom{n}{i} \theta_L^i (1 - \theta_L)^{n-i} = (1 - \gamma)/2$$
$$\sum_{i=0}^{X} \binom{n}{i} \theta_U^i (1 - \theta_U)^{n-i} = (1 + \gamma)/2. \tag{1.14}$$

Reliability and Conditional Standard Error of Measurement

In strong true score theory, reliability is still the ratio of true score variance to observed score variance. Although strong true score theory is not developed in the same manner as classical test theory, it leads to some of the same reliability estimates as classical test theory, such as the Kuder-Richardson formula 20 and 21 (Kuder & Richardson, 1937). Chapter 4 discusses these estimates in more detail.

In strong true score theory, the binomial distribution provides a relatively easy method for obtaining examinee-specific error variances (i.e., error variance conditional on true score). The binomial distribution has a variance of $n\theta(1 - \theta)$ (see Hogg & Tanis, 2001), and Lord (1955b) showed that when adopting the notion of sampling items from a domain, this formula was the error variance for a given score. By transforming the domain score to the raw score metric and denoting it by τ, domain scores take on a value between 0 and the total number of items, n. The variance of the binomial distribution may then be expressed as $\tau(n - \tau)/n$. Keats (1957) improved upon this estimator by incorporating a small sample correction to obtain $\tau(n - \tau)/(n - 1)$. He also multiplied this value by the adjustment factor $(1 - \rho_{XT}^2)/(1 - r_{21})$ to account for small differences in item difficulty. Taking the square root of this conditional error variance results in an estimate of the standard error of measurement conditional on true score,

$$CSEM(\tau) = \sqrt{\frac{1 - \rho_{XT}^2}{1 - r_{21}} \frac{\tau(n - \tau)}{n - 1}}. \tag{1.15}$$

Keats further demonstrated that the average value of the conditional error variance was equal to the standard error of measurement in classical test theory. To compute the conditional standard error of measurement, an estimate of reliability is substituted for ρ_{XT}^2. The important implication of Equation 1.15 is that error variance may be computed for specific score levels. This contrasts with classical test theory, in which all examinees are assigned the same error variance (see Equation 1.5), regardless of their true score.

This section introduced squared error and threshold loss methods for evaluating reliability in criterion-referenced tests. Decision consistency and decision accuracy were defined, and strong true score concepts necessary for estimating these quantities from a single replication were briefly discussed. The methods presented in this section suffer from the same weakness as classical test theory: Only one source of error is reflected in a single estimate. Multiple sources of error can only be considered simultaneously using generalizability theory.

Generalizability Theory

A reliability analysis conducted via generalizability theory consists of two distinct steps, and each step consists of its own terminology and concepts. The first step is a generalizability study, and its purpose is to identify important characteristics of the measurement procedure and evaluate the amount of score variability attributed to each characteristic. The second step is a decision study, and its purpose is to determine the dependability of scores obtained from a measurement procedure and possibly design more efficient measurement procedures.

Generalizability Study

In the discussion of classical test theory, two types of sampling were described: sampling of examinees and replicating the measurement procedure. These types of sampling are more formally integrated into generalizability theory, and, as discussed in Chapter 3, the sampling is assumed to be random. The *population* defines characteristics of the objects of measurement that may be sampled for participation in the measurement procedure. Examinees typically constitute the object of measurement, but generalizability theory permits other entities, such as expert performance raters, to be the object of measurement. In what follows, examinees are the objects of measurement. A desirable source of score variability arises from sampling examinees from the population. Undesirable sources of variability result from the process of sampling other aspects of the measurement procedure.

Sampling (i.e., replicating) the measurement procedure contributes to measurement error. Classical test theory and strong true score theory only permit one source of sampling in addition to the sampling of examinees. Therefore, only one source of measurement error may be considered at any one time. Generalizability theory, on the other hand, allows sampling from multiple sources in addition to sampling examinees. This multifaceted sampling permits error to be partitioned into multiple sources and the influence of each or all sources, as well as their interactions, may be considered simultaneously. To properly conduct or conceptualize this multifaceted sampling, the sampling frame must be clearly defined.

Sources of measurement error are referred to as *facets* in generalizability theory. Test items are an example of an item facet. The occasion in which a measurement procedure is conducted (e.g., morning, afternoon, and evening administrations) constitutes an occasion facet. A measurement procedure may have one facet or many facets. The number of facets selected depends on the major sources of error present in a measurement procedure. However, it is wise to select only those sources of measurement error that are likely to have the greatest impact on scores. Model complexity increases exponentially as the number of facets increases. The *universe of admissible observations* refers to all of the facets from which samples may be drawn in order to create an instance of the measurement procedure. It is a sampling frame that specifies the characteristics of every facet that may be included in a measurement procedure.

In a *generalizability study*, the population and universe of admissible observations are defined, as well as the observed universe design. A design specifies (a) the organization of the facets, (b) the facet sample size, and (c) the size of the universe. When discussing design considerations for the generalizability study, the phrase "observed universe design" or "observed design" is used to indicate the design that resulted in actual data. It reflects the characteristics of an observed measurement procedure. An observed design pertains to the universe of admissible observations and is part of the generalizability study because the data are used to estimate variance components for individual observations of each facet. Design considerations in the dependability study, discussed later, are referred to as the *data collection design*. This distinction is important because, in the generalizability study, the design pertains to single observations (e.g., a single item), but it refers to a collection of observations (e.g., a group of items) in the dependability study. Moreover, the observed design and data collection design may be the same or they may be different.

Observed designs may involve a single facet or multiple facets. A design with a single facet is referred to as a *single-facet design*. One with two facets is referred to as a *two-facet design*. Designs with more than two facets are referenced in a similar manner. Once a number of facets have been specified, aspects of their organization must be described.

A facet is *crossed* with another facet when two or more conditions of one facet are observed with each condition of another

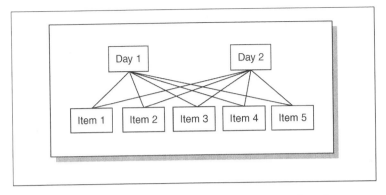

Figure 1.7. Diagram of Items Crossed with Occasions (i.e., Day of Administration)

facet. Consider a design that involves an item facet and an occasion facet. When all items are administered on all occasions, the item and occasion facets are crossed (see Fig. 1.7). Crossing is denoted with a multiplication sign. For example, "Item × Occasion" would be read as "item crossed with occasion." This notation may be simplified to $i \times o$. (Note that this text uses Brennan's [2001b] notational conventions). A facet may also be crossed with the object of measurement. When all objects of measurement, say examinees, respond to all items, examinees and items are crossed. This design would be denoted as $p \times i$, where p refers to examinees (i.e., persons). Data collection designs in which all facets and objects of measurement are crossed are referred to as *fully crossed designs.*

Cronbach noted that generalizability theory's strength lies in its ability to specify designs that are not fully crossed (Cronbach & Shavelson, 2004). A *nested* facet (call it A) occurs when (a) two or more conditions of A are observed with each condition of another facet (referred to as B), and (b) each condition of B contains different levels of A (Shavelson & Webb, 1991, p. 46). For example, suppose a measurement procedure is conducted on two occasions, and a different set of items is administered on each occasion. Items are nested within occasion (see Fig. 1.8). Nesting is denoted with a colon. For example, "Items : Occasion" would be read as "items nested within occasion." For brevity, this relationship may also be denoted as $i : o$. A facet may also be nested within the object of

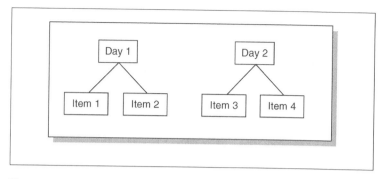

Figure 1.8. Diagram of Items Nested Within Occasion (i.e., Day of Administration)

measurement. For example, items are nested within examinees if each examinee is given a different set of test items, a situation commonly encountered in computerized adaptive testing (see van der Linden & Glass, 2000). This design may be denoted $i : p$. Designs that do not involve any crossed facets are referred to as nested or *fully nested designs*. Those that involve a combination of nested and crossed facets are referred to as *partially nested designs*.

Facet sample sizes are specified in the observed design strictly for the purposes of observing a measurement procedure and obtaining data. These sample sizes are denoted with a lowercase n with a subscript that represents the facet. For example, the observed sample size for the item facet is denoted n_i. The linear model effects and the variance components in a generalizability study (described below) refer to facet sample sizes of 1. For example, a measurement procedure may be observed by administering a 64-item test to 2,000 examinees. Every examinee responds to the same 64 items. Therefore, this design is crossed. Variance components estimated in the generalizability study from this data refer to variance attributable to a single item or the interaction of an examinee and a single item. The data collection design in the decision study (discussed later) specifies facet sample sizes for the purpose of estimating error variance and reliability for a collection of elements from a facet (i.e., a group of test items). Facet sample sizes play a greater role in the decision study.

When defining the observed design, the size of the universe must be considered. *Random* universes are unrestricted and larger than the particular conditions included in a measurement procedure. An item facet is random if the items that appear on a test are randomly sampled from, or considered exchangeable with, all possible items that could have been included on the test. The ELA item pool scenario described earlier is an example. In that scenario, a 50-item ELA test was created from an item pool of 200 items. The item pool serves as the universe and the 50 selected items are part of a specific instance of the measurement procedure. Presumably the 50 items were selected at random or the test designer is willing to exchange any one of the 50 items for any other item in the pool. In this case, the item facet is considered to be random. Conversely, *fixed* universes are restricted to those conditions that are actually included in the measurement procedure. For example, the item facet is fixed if there was no item pool and the 50 ELA items were considered to exhaust all of the items in the universe. The difference between random and fixed universes is more than a semantic one. Each implies a different generalization and interpretation of score reliability.

An observed universe design may be characterized using a linear model, and many different models are possible in generalizability theory. Each model decomposes a single examinee's score on single observations of the facets. Three designs will be considered in this text: $p \times i$, $p \times i \times o$, and $p \times (i : o)$. In the $p \times i$ design, all examinees respond to all items. The score for an examinee on a single item, X_{pi}, is the sum of four parts,

$$X_{pi} = \mu + v_p + v_i + v_{pi}, \qquad (1.16)$$

where μ refers to the grand mean (i.e., average score over all examinees and all facets), v_p refers to the person effect, and v_i refers to the item effect. The term v_{pi} reflects the interaction between persons and items. However, this latter effect is confounded with the residual, given that there is only one observation per cell. This effect is due to the interaction of the person and item, as well as any other random source of error not reflected in the design. Because of this confounding, it is referred to as the *residual effect*.

The notation used here is not entirely descriptive of the effects in the linear model. For example, the item effect is actually $v_i = \mu_i - \mu$. The shortened versions of these effects are used herein for brevity and to reduce the technical aspects as much as possible to facilitate an understanding of reliability. The complete linear models are described in Brennan (2001b) and Shavelson and Webb (1991).

A $p \times i \times o$ design with an item and occasion facet requires that all examinees respond to all items on all occasions. Scores are described as

$$X_{pio} = \mu + v_p + v_i + v_o + v_{pi} + v_{po} + v_{io} + v_{pio}. \qquad (1.17)$$

Effects due to person, item, and the person-by-item interaction are the same as stated previously. The effect due to occasion is v_o. Two-way interactions between person and occasion, v_{po}, and item and occasion, v_{io}, and the three-way interaction between person, item, and occasion, v_{pio} are also part of this model.

Finally, a score from a two-facet design with items nested within occasion, $p \times (i : o)$, is characterized by

$$X_{pio} = \mu + v_p + v_o + v_{i:o} + v_{po} + v_{pi:o}. \qquad (1.18)$$

Nesting items within occasion reduces the number of effects that influence scores. There are only five effects in this model but seven effects in the two-facet fully crossed design.

Variance Components. A generalizability study is conducted to estimate the amount of score variance associated with each effect in the universe of admissible observations. Each effect in the linear model has its own variance component. That is, total score variability is decomposed into variance due to each effect and their interactions. In the $p \times i$ design, the variance components are

$$\sigma^2(X_{pi}) = \sigma^2(p) + \sigma^2(i) + \sigma^2(pi). \qquad (1.19)$$

Item variance, $\sigma^2(i)$, reflects the extent to which items vary in difficulty. Variance due to the person-by-item interaction, $\sigma^2(pi)$, indicates variability associated with items that are difficult for some examinees yet easy for others. Finally, $\sigma^2(p)$ indicates the amount of variability among examinees due to the underlying construct. Each of these effects is found in the more elaborate two-facet crossed design.

Variance components for the $p \times i \times o$ design are

$$\sigma^2(X_{pio}) = \sigma^2(p) + \sigma^2(i) + \sigma^2(o) + \sigma^2(pi) + \sigma^2(po)$$
$$+ \sigma^2(io) + \sigma^2(pio). \tag{1.20}$$

Scores may be higher on some occasions than others. Variability of scores due to occasion is reflected in $\sigma^2(o)$. Item difficulty may vary depending on occasion. That is, items may be difficult on one occasion but easy on another. This source of variability is reflected in $\sigma^2(io)$. Variance for the person-by-occasion interaction, $\sigma^2(po)$, is interpreted similarly; variability of examinee performance from one occasion to another. Finally, variance due to the interaction of persons, items, and occasions, as well as any remaining source of random error, is reflected in the residual term, $\sigma^2(pio)$.

The $p \times (i : o)$ design consists of fewer variance components than the $p \times i \times o$ due to nesting. These components are

$$\sigma^2(X_{pio}) = \sigma^2(p) + \sigma^2(o) + \sigma^2(i : o) + \sigma^2(po) + \sigma^2(pi : o). \tag{1.21}$$

The two components unique to this design are $\sigma^2(i : o)$ and $\sigma^2(pi : o)$. The former term reflects variability of item difficulty within an occasion. The latter term corresponds to the interaction between persons and items nested within occasion, as well as other sources of random variability. That is, $\sigma^2(pi : o)$ is also a residual term.

In a generalizability study, variance components are estimated using ANOVA methods. Estimates are then interpreted in a relative manner by computing the proportion of variance explained by each component (i.e., the ratio of one source of variance to the total variance). Examples of these computations will be provided later. Variance component estimates are used in a decision study to evaluate the dependability of scores and to design efficient measurement procedures.

Decision Study

Scores in a generalizability study reflect the contribution of single observations of each facet. In the $p \times i$ design, the score X_{pi} is a person's score on an individual item. In the $p \times i \times o$ design, the score X_{pio} is a person's score on a single item on a single occasion. Variance components estimated in a generalizability study tell us how much each facet and facet interaction contributes to variability of these "single observation" scores. In practice, tests are rarely composed of a single item or a single item administered on a single occasion. Rather, scores are based on a collection of items or a collection of items obtained from a collection of occasions. A *decision study* provides the framework for evaluating the dependability of scores obtained by averaging over a collection of facets. More importantly, the *universe of generalization* is defined in a decision study by specifying the number of observations of each facet that constitutes a replication of the measurement procedure and other details of the data collection design.

The number of observations of each facet (i.e., the items facet sample size) is denoted in the same way as the facet sample size in the observed design, but a prime mark is added. For example, the item facet sample size is denoted n_i'. The prime is added because the sample size in the decision study may differ from the sample size in the observed design.

A decision study allows one to evaluate the reliability of different data collection designs that may be the same as or different from the observed design. Decision study facet sample sizes may be the same as or different from the actual sample sizes used when implementing the measurement procedure in a generalizability study. For example, a 60-item test may have been administered to examinees when conducting the generalizability study ($n_i = 60$), but a researcher may be interested in evaluating the reliability of a shorter 45-item test in the decision study ($n_i' = 45$). As another example, suppose a 60-item test is administered over a two-day period (30 items per day), but the researcher notices examinees experiencing notable fatigue during testing each day. Data from the two-day testing could be used in a decision study to evaluate the reliability of extending testing to four days, but reducing the number of items per day to 15. A decision study allows one to consider various data collection designs, as well as different ways to organize the facets.

A variety of methods for organizing facets may be evaluated in a decision study. For example, a $p \times i$ observed design may be used to evaluate a $p \times I$ or an $I : p$ data collection design (use of the capital letter I will be explained shortly). Or, a $p \times i \times o$ observed design may be used to evaluate a $p \times I \times O$, $p \times (I : O)$, or $I : O : p$ data collection design. The number of possible data collection designs is not unlimited, however. Nested facets in the generalizability study cannot be crossed in the decision study. An $i : p$ generalizability study cannot be used to conduct a $p \times I$ decision study. Therefore, a generalizability study should be conducted with as many facets crossed as possible.

The size of the universe of generalization may be the same as or different from the universe of admissible observations. An infinite (i.e., random) facet in the universe of admissible observations may be fixed in the universe of generalization as long as there is at least one random facet in the design. The converse is not true. A fixed facet in the universe of admissible observations may not be made infinite in the universe of generalization. Therefore, to have the most flexibility in conducting a decision study, the generalizability study should be conducted with as many random facets as possible.

Linear models in a decision study reflect the composite nature of scores. For example, the linear model for the $p \times I$ design with n_i' items is given by

$$X_{pI} = \mu + v_p + v_I + v_{pI}. \tag{1.22}$$

The score X_{pI} refers to an average score over n_i' items. The capital letter I denotes an average over the n_i' items. More generally, a capitalized facet index indicates an average over that facet (see Brennan, 2001b). This notation is intentional, and it distinguishes a decision study linear model from a generalizability study linear model. Each effect in the model is interpreted with respect to the collection of observations for each facet. The item effect, v_I, refers to the effect of n_i' items (i.e., a test form), and the person-by-item interaction refers to the differential effect of test forms for examinees. Linear models for the two facet designs are adjusted in a similar manner.

In the $p \times I \times O$ design, an examinee's average score from n'_i items and n'_o occasions is given by

$$X_{pIO} = \mu + v_p + v_I + v_O + v_{pI} + v_{pI} + v_{IO} + v_{pIO}. \qquad (1.23)$$

Nesting items within occasion reduces the total number of effects in the decision study linear model, just as it did in the generalizability study linear model. In the $p \times (I : O)$ design, an examinee's average score from n'_i items that are nested within n'_o occasions is

$$X_{pIO} = \mu + v_p + v_O + v_{I:O} + v_{pO} + v_{pI:O}. \qquad (1.24)$$

Each of these linear models shows that observed scores are comprised of a number of effects, all of which influence scores upon each replication of the measurement procedure.

Replicating the Measurement Procedure. The universe of generalization includes all possible randomly parallel instances of a measurement procedure. For example, a universe of generalization may involve all possible 60-item eighth grade mathematics test forms that could be administered to every examinee. Another universe of generalization may involve all possible 30-item sixth grade ELA test forms that could be administered on one day, and all possible 30-item sixth grade ELA test forms that could be administered on a second day. Each particular instance of the universe of generalization constitutes a replication of the measurement procedure. For example, one 60-item eighth grade mathematics test administered to all examinees is one replication of the measurement procedure. A second 60-item eighth grade mathematics test administered to all examinees is another replication of the measurement procedure. As in classical test theory, the score a person obtains from one replication will differ from the score obtained on another replication because of random error (i.e., sampling from each facet). However, in generalizability theory, scores observed in each replication are affected by multiple sources of error, not just a single source of error, as in classical test theory. All of the terms in Equations 1.22, 1.23, and 1.24 except μ and v_p may be thought of as error scores. However, the exclusion of μ and ν_p does not imply that these two effects are true scores.

Generalizability theory does not make use of true scores as they were defined in classical test theory. A similar concept exists, and it depends on the definition of a universe of generalization. A *universe score* is the average of all possible observed scores a person would obtain from every possible randomly parallel replication of the measurement procedure. For example, imagine that a random sample of 60 mathematics items were given to an examinee, and the examinee's average score was computed. Suppose then that another random sample of 60 mathematics items was selected and administered to the examinee and another average score was computed. Repeating the process of randomly sampling items and computing an average score a large number of times would result in a distribution of observed scores. The universe score would be the average value of all of these scores. A histogram of these scores would look similar to Figure 1.2, but the x-axis would be average scores, not sum scores.

In generalizability theory, we seek to determine how well an observed score *generalizes* to the universe score in the universe of generalization (Brennan, 2001b). This notion explains the use of the term "generalizability" in generalizability theory. To evaluate this generalization, the amount of variance associated with observed scores must be determined. If observed score variance is primarily due to universe score variance (i.e., the variance of universe scores among a sample of examinees), then observed scores may be reliably generalized to universe scores. That is, we can have confidence that observed scores are close to universe scores. Contrarily, if observed score variance is mostly due to error variance, then observed scores will not reliably generalize to universe scores, and we cannot have confidence that observed scores are close to universe scores.

Sources of Variance. It is well known in statistics that if scores $x_1, x_2, \ldots, x_n$ are independently and identically distributed with a given mean, μ, and variance, σ^2, then the distribution of the average of these scores, $\bar{x} = 1/n \sum_{i=1}^{n} x_i$, has a mean μ and variance σ^2/n (see Hogg & Tanis, 2001). That is, the variance for an average score is the variance for the individual score divided by the sample size. This result is commonly encountered in statistics classes, where it is known as the *standard error*. It also plays an important role in a decision study.

Variance components estimated in a generalizability study pertain to individual observations, and these components are used to estimate variance components for an average of observations in a decision study. Therefore, a decision study variance component is usually the generalizability study variance component divided by the facet sample size. ("Usually," because in some designs, multiple generalizability study variance components are combined before division by the sample size.) An obvious result of dividing a variance component by the facet sample size is that the amount of variance decreases. Consider the variance components for the $p \times I$ design, which are given by

$$\sigma^2(X_{pI}) = \sigma^2(p) + \frac{\sigma^2(i)}{n'_i} + \frac{\sigma^2(pi)}{n'_i}. \tag{1.25}$$

Three sources of variance are evident in this equation. Universe score variance is denoted $\sigma^2(p)$, and it indicates the amount that scores vary due to real differences among examinees. Variance attributed to the group of n'_i items (i.e., a test form) and the person-by-form interaction is reflected in the remaining two terms on the right-hand side. More importantly, these latter terms represent two sources of error variance that decrease as the number of items increases.

Increasing the number of facets increases the sources of error variance, as is evident in the $p \times I \times O$ design. Seven sources of variance comprise the total observed score variance,

$$\sigma^2(X_{pIO}) = \sigma^2(p) + \frac{\sigma^2(i)}{n'_i} + \frac{\sigma^2(o)}{n'_o} + \frac{\sigma^2(pi)}{n'_i} + \frac{\sigma^2(po)}{n'_o}$$
$$+ \frac{\sigma^2(io)}{n'_i n'_o} + \frac{\sigma^2(pio)}{n'_i n'_o}. \tag{1.26}$$

One source is universe score variance, while the others are sources of error variance. Notice that variance for interacting facets are divided by the product of two facet sample sizes. Therefore, increasing a facet sample size not only reduces variance for that facet, but also other variance terms that involve that facet.

Similar observations can be made among the $p \times (I : O)$ design variance components,

$$\sigma^2(X_{pIO}) = \sigma^2(p) + \frac{\sigma^2(o)}{n'_o} + \frac{\sigma^2(i:o)}{n'_i n'_o} + \frac{\sigma^2(po)}{n'_o} + \frac{\sigma^2(pi:o)}{n'_i n'_o}. \quad (1.27)$$

Universe score variance and four sources of error variance are evident in this design. Although there are fewer sources of error variance in the $p \times (I : O)$ than in the $p \times I \times O$, it is not necessarily true the total amount of variance will be smaller in the former design than the latter.

Types of Decisions. At the beginning of the section on classification decisions, relative and absolute score scales were discussed. A relative method of scaling compares one examinee's scores to another examinee's score. Absolute scaling compares an examinee's score to some standard, such as a cut-score. The decision to use one scaling method or another depends on the type of decision a test user must make. A *relative decision* involves a relative method of scaling for the purpose of deciding which examinees score higher (or lower) than others. For example, an employer may want to use a job placement test to select the most qualified applicant. Scores on this test should do a good job of rank ordering examinees, so that the highest-scoring examinee may be selected for the job. An *absolute decision* involves an absolute method of scaling for the purpose of deciding whether examinees have met or have failed to meet some standard. No rank ordering is involved, as all examinees may be above or below the standard. For example, a licensing board may want use a test to determine whether or not examinees meet some minimum standard of proficiency. Scores on the test are used to decide who is proficient and who is not. For granting a license, it does not matter if one examinee scores higher than another, as long as both are above the standard.

Generalizability theory formally integrates the type of decision into measurement error. Important sources of error for relative decisions are those that affect the rank ordering of examinees. These sources of error involve the interaction between a facet and the object of measurement because they disrupt the ordering of examinees. That is, an effect may increase scores for some examinees, but decrease scores for others. Table 1.2 lists relative error for the three designs under consideration. Notice that the sources of error that constitute relative error are those that involve the object of measurement index and one or more facet index. Relative error is denoted with a lowercase Greek letter delta, δ. Variance for relative error is denoted $\sigma^2(\delta)$.

Important sources of error for absolute decisions are those that affect the ordering of examinees and the absolute standing of examinees. These sources of error involve the interactions and the main effects. Interactions affect scores in the manner described in the previous paragraph, which may cause some examinees to be above the cut-score and some to be below. Main effects shift scores up or down for all examinees, possibly moving all scores above or below a cut-score. Given that relative and absolute shifts in scores affect the absolute standing of examinees, absolute error tends to be larger than relative error. This result is evident in Table 1.2. Absolute error terms involve more sources of error than relative error terms. Absolute error is denoted with an uppercase Greek letter delta, Δ. Absolute error variance is denoted $\sigma^2(\Delta)$.

Reliability Coefficients. There are two types of reliability coefficients in generalizability theory. The *generalizability coefficient* was introduced by Cronbach and associates (1963) when generalizability theory was first introduced. This coefficient describes the reliability of scores used for relative decisions. It is the ratio of universe score variance to universe score variance plus relative error variance,

$$\epsilon\rho^2 = \frac{\sigma^2(p)}{\sigma^2(p) + \sigma^2(\delta)}. \tag{1.28}$$

Note that ϵ denotes mathematical expectation. Equation 1.28 really describes a family of coefficients, with each member characterized by a different expression for relative error. For example,

Table 1.2
Relative and Absolute Error for Three Random Designs

Variance	Design	Expression
Universe Score	All	$\sigma^2(p) = \sigma^2(p)$
Relative Error	$p \times I$	$\sigma^2(\delta) = \frac{\sigma^2(pi)}{n'_i}$
	$p \times I \times O$	$\sigma^2(\delta) = \frac{\sigma^2(pi)}{n'_i} + \frac{\sigma^2(po)}{n'_o} + \frac{\sigma^2(pio)}{n'_i n'_o}$
	$p \times I : O$	$\sigma^2(\delta) = \frac{\sigma^2(po)}{n'_o} + \frac{\sigma^2(pio)}{n'_i n'_o}$
Absolute Error	$p \times I$	$\sigma^2(\Delta) = \frac{\sigma^2(i)}{n'_i} + \frac{\sigma^2(pi)}{n'_i}$
	$p \times I \times O$	$\sigma^2(\Delta) = \frac{\sigma^2(i)}{n'_i} + \frac{\sigma^2(o)}{n'_o} + \frac{\sigma^2(pi)}{n'_i}$ $+ \frac{\sigma^2(po)}{n'_o} + \frac{\sigma^2(io)}{n'_i n'_o} + \frac{\sigma^2(pio)}{n'_i n'_o}$
	$p \times I : O$	$\sigma^2(\Delta) = \frac{\sigma^2(i:o)}{n'_i} + \frac{\sigma^2(o)}{n'_o} + \frac{\sigma^2(po)}{n'_o} + \frac{\sigma^2(pio)}{n'_i n'_o}$

each design in Table 1.2 has its own expression for relative error, hence its own generalizability coefficient.

Absolute decisions differ from relative decisions, as described earlier. Brennan and Kane (1977) defined the *index of dependability* to describe the reliability of scores used for absolute decisions. It represents the ratio of universe score variance to universe score variance plus absolute error variance,

$$\Phi = \frac{\sigma^2(p)}{\sigma^2(p) + \sigma^2(\Delta)}. \tag{1.29}$$

Because of the notation used to introduce this index, it is also referred to as the *phi coefficient* (Φ). Like the generalizability coefficient, the Φ coefficient represents a family of reliability coefficients in which each member of the family is characterized by a different term for absolute error.

In generalizability theory, the selected coefficient should match the type of decision a test user is making. A generalizability coefficient should be used for relative decisions and a Φ coefficient should be used for absolute decisions. Although this seems to go without saying, the magnitude of each coefficient will usually differ, making it tempting to report the larger of the two. Generalizability coefficients are usually larger than Φ coefficients because of the smaller error term in the ratio. However, it is not appropriate to report a generalizability coefficient for test scores used to make absolute decisions. Sometimes both types of decisions are made. Educational tests are an example. Many states report test scores as well as achievement levels. In this situation, estimates of both coefficients should be reported, not just the larger of the two.

Estimating Unobserved Quantities. Variance components are estimated with ANOVA methods, as explained in Brennan (2001b) and Shavelson and Webb (1991). These estimates are then substituted into the expression for relative or absolute error. The standard error of measurement is estimated by taking the square root of the expression for relative or absolute error that is applicable for a given data collection design. A relative standard error of measurement is $\sqrt{\sigma^2(\delta)}$ and an absolute standard error of measurement is $\sqrt{\sigma^2(\Delta)}$. Examples of these computations are provided later.

The flexibility of generalizability theory should be evident even in this short introduction. It liberalizes reliability concepts from classical test theory by allowing multiple sources of error to be considered simultaneously. Although not discussed herein, generalizability theory also extends to tests comprised of multiple factors. However, multivariate generalizability theory is rather complicated and beyond the scope of this text.

Data collection designs are discussed in more detail in the next chapter, and the primary assumptions in generalizability theory are described in Chapter 3. Example computations and example write-ups follow in subsequent chapters.

Chapter Summary

The chapter began by stressing the importance of reliability in the social sciences and the impact of reliability on the quality of test scores, statistical analysis, and score validation. General concepts that cut across classical test theory, classification decisions, and generalizability theory were described, and an overview of these three approaches to score reliability was provided. This review was not exhaustive by any means, and the reader is encouraged to consult additional sources. It is hoped that by emphasizing the notion of replicating the measurement procedure, the reader understands that there is no one reliability coefficient and no single interpretation of reliability. The entire measurement procedure and how it is replicated should be considered to identify important sources of error, quantify the impact of error on test scores, and interpret a reliability coefficient.

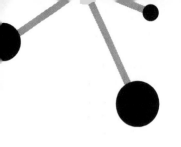

2

DATA COLLECTION DESIGNS

DATA COLLECTION DESIGNS in measurement fit the framework of within-subjects factorial designs (see Keppel & Wickens, 2004). Designs for classical test theory and classification decisions are limited to a two-factor design. Examinees (i.e., the object of measurement) always represent one factor in the design, and a source of measurement error represents the other. The particular source of error may differ, but only one source is characterized by a design.

Generalizability theory builds on the factorial nature of a data collection design and allows a single design to incorporate multiple sources of error. It also allows the sources of error to be organized in different ways. For example, a single design may involve two sources of error: items and occasions. These sources may be organized as crossed or nested. Items and occasions are crossed if every item is administered on every occasion. Items are nested within occasions if a different set of items is administered on each occasion. The factorial nature of a data collection design permits a measurement procedure to be characterized in numerous ways.

A data collection design is chosen to isolate a source of error and achieve a particular interpretation of a reliability estimate. For example, the influence of time on observed scores may be evaluated by taking measurements on the same examinees at two time points. With a carefully chosen time interval between the two measurements, the main source of changes in the observed scores for each examinee is the lack of stability in the construct of interest. Moreover, the appropriate interpretation of a reliability estimate based on this design is as a coefficient of stability. Interpreting this estimate as a coefficient of equivalence is inappropriate. The data collection design isolates a particular source or sources of error and guides the interpretation of a reliability estimate.

The next section describes a real-world measurement procedure that will form the basis of many examples in this chapter. Subsequent sections describe data collection designs commonly encountered in measurement. Classical test theory designs are organized according to how the measurement procedure is replicated. Designs involving two whole-test replications and two or more part-test replications are described. Designs in generalizability theory are organized according to the number and organization of facets. All designs are revisited in Chapter 4, when various methods for estimating reliability are discussed.

Description of Real-world Measurement Procedure

The South Carolina Benchmark Testing Program consists of the Benchmark Assessments of student learning and professional development opportunities for teachers. Assessments cover the state curriculum standards, a comprehensive set of learning goals and objectives, for English Language Arts (ELA) and mathematics. The Benchmarks are administered in the fall and spring to provide teachers with feedback on student progress during the academic year. Each test administration is followed by professional development activities that help teachers interpret test scores and adapt curricula and instruction for student needs. The goal of the Benchmark program is to improve classroom instruction and student performance.

The ELA Benchmarks for eighth grade are aligned to the 2002 ELA standards (see Table 2.1; South Carolina Department of Education, 2002). The first three strands (i.e., Reading 1, 2, and 3) tap into reading comprehension and have the following goal: "The student will draw upon a variety of strategies to comprehend, interpret, analyze, and evaluate what he or she reads" (p. 156). The

Table 2.1

English Language Arts (ELA) Curriculum Standards and Percentage of Items in Each Standard for Grade Eight

Strand	Description	Form A	Form B
Reading 1	The student will integrate various cues and strategies to comprehend what he or she reads.	44	31
Reading 2	The student will use a knowledge of the purposes, structures, and elements of writing to analyze and interpret various types of texts.	31	38
Reading 3	The student will use a knowledge of semantics, syntax, and structural analysis to determine the meaning of unfamiliar words and read texts with understanding.	6	9
Research 1	The student will select a topic for exploration.	9	3
Research 2	The student will gather information from a variety of sources.	9	19

last two strands, listed in Table 2.1, involve research and are based on the goal: "The student will access and use information from a variety of appropriately selected sources to extend his or her knowledge" (p. 171). Each strand is further subdivided into standards that identify the specific aspects of what students should know and be able to do, but, for brevity, the standards are not listed herein.

Example reliability computations and write-ups involve the fall administration of the grade eight test of ELA. This particular test emphasizes reading comprehension, and it consists of eight testlets of eight questions for a total of 64 items. Testlets are a subset of items that are related by a common feature, such as a reading passage or graphic (Wainer & Kiely, 1987). For the ELA assessment, the testlets are formed around a common reading passage. All 64 questions are not administered on the same day. Rather, the first four testlets are administered on day one and the second four are administered the next day. Schools had a two-week window to administer the assessment resulting in variability of when the two occasions were observed.

Data Collections Designs in Classical Test Theory

Data collection designs in classical test theory always involve a two-factor design. Only one factor represents a source of measurement error, but the particular source of error differs according to the manner in which the measurement procedure is replicated. For example, one type of replication may involve administering a test to a group of examinees, allowing a few weeks to pass, then administering the same test to the same examinees. Another type of replication may involve administering two different (although very similar) test forms to the same examinees on two occasions. Each type of replication involves a two-factor design, but the source of error is different. There are many ways to define a replication, even when restricted to a two-factor design. Defining a replication begins with deciding whether to use a whole-test or part-test replication. Test-retest, alternate forms, and test-retest with alternate forms all use whole-test replications.

Whole Test Replications

Test-Retest Reliability Coefficient. Reliability coefficients estimated by two whole-test replications include test-retest, alternate forms, and test-retest with alternate forms. In the test-retest design, scores obtained by administering the same test on two different occasions are compared. Table 2.2 outlines the data collection design. Error variance in this design is due to random temporal fluctuations of the characteristic being measured, as well as to changes in other attributes such as such as alertness, forgetfulness, distractibility, hunger, and guessing. Differences in the test administration, such as different testing rooms or different

Table 2.2

Data Collection Design for Test-Retest Reliability

Person	Occasion 1	Occasion 2
P1	Form A	Form A
P2	Form A	Form A
P3	Form A	Form A
P4	Form A	Form A

administration times, may also contribute to error variance. If observed scores substantially fluctuate from one occasion to another because of random temporal fluctuations among examinee characteristics, the observed scores will not be stable. On the other hand, if there is very little random variation among examinee characteristics from one occasion to another, observed scores will be stable over time. The test-retest reliability coefficient is known as a *coefficient of stability*. It reflects the extent to which observed scores provide stable estimates of true scores (over time).

Proper interpretation of the test-retest reliability coefficient depends on the time interval between the two administrations of the measurement. Choosing an appropriate time interval is a fine balance between making it long enough to avoid the introduction of additional sources of error and short enough to avoid having examinees change in a systematic way on the characteristic of interest.

Practice effects and fatigue are two potential sources of problems with test-retest reliability estimates. If examinees remember their first responses to items when responding to them a second time, the error scores from the two administrations will be related and violate a basic assumption of the classical test score model. Gulliksen (1950, p. 197) notes that this effect will result in a reliability estimate that is larger than it should be. However, his statement does not take into account other, possibly contradictory, effects, such as the influence of fatigue.

The test-retest method requires examinees to take the same test twice, which doubles the amount of testing time. Fatigue caused by such an extended testing period will systematically alter examinee performance (i.e., modify true scores due to a bias among error scores). Lord and Novick (1968) note that for the test-retest reliability coefficient, such an effect introduces additional error and lowers the estimate of reliability. Taken together, fatigue and practice effects do not cancel out each other, and their combined influence on the test-retest reliability coefficient is unknown (Lord & Novick). Nevertheless, one must carefully consider the time interval between measurements. It should be long enough to avoid practice effects and fatigue, yet short enough to avoid having the examinee develop or systematically change on the characteristic being measured.

Systematic changes among true scores may also occur in pre-post research designs. Therefore, test-retest reliability is not an appropriate reliability coefficient for this situation. In a *pre-post design*, examinees participate in the first measurement administration, some sort of intervention designed to systematically alter the characteristic being measured is introduced, and a second measurement is conducted. For example, suppose a researcher has developed a new method for teaching reading comprehension. This researcher recruits students for a study designed to evaluate the amount that reading comprehension improves due to the new teaching method. After completing a measure of reading comprehension, the students participate in the new instructional method every day during school for four months. At the end of this time period, the students complete the same measure of reading comprehension. If the researcher's hypothesis is supported, students will systematically improve their scores on the reading comprehension test. The observed score variance is likely to change as well. In this situation, the characteristic being measured changes systematically as a result of the new teaching method. Test-retest is sensitive to random variation among observed scores, provided that true scores do not change systematically from one replication of the measurement to another. When true scores are expected to change as a result of some type of intervention, test-retest is not an appropriate reliability coefficient. If it is used, the reliability estimate will be smaller than it should be (Lord & Novick, 1968, p. 134).

The time interval between occasions should be reported whenever a test-retest reliability estimate is reported, given its influence on the reliability estimate. Only those estimates based on the same time interval are comparable. For example, a test-retest reliability estimate of 0.60 obtained by administering the measure two weeks apart does not permit the same interpretation of the same size estimate that was obtained by administering the measures three months apart. Stated differently, a two-week test retest estimate reflects a different method of replicating the measurement procedure than a three-month test-retest reliability estimate.

Alternate Forms Reliability Coefficient. When reliability is estimated by having examinees take two whole-test replications, each on a different occasion, the influence of practice effects may be reduced by using a different test form for each occasion. In this design, scores on each form are compared. The time interval between measurement administrations is typically shorter than the time intervals used when estimating test-retest reliability, but it should be long enough to minimize fatigue. Counterbalancing the order in which forms are administered eliminates the influence of occasion (i.e., time or stability of the characteristic being measured). Forms may be counterbalanced by administering one form to half of the examinees and the other form to the remaining examinees during the first occasion. Examinees then respond to the alternate form on the second occasion. Consider the ELA Benchmark assessment for an example. Form A and Form B of this measure are designed to be very similar. Suppose that half of the examinees complete Form A on the first occasion and Form B on the second occasion, and the other half of the examinees do the opposite. An outline of this design is shown in Table 2.3.

Table 2.3

Data Collection Design for Alternate Forms Reliability with Counterbalancing

Person	Occasion 1	Occasion 2
P1	Form A	Form B
P2	Form A	Form B
P3	Form B	Form A
P4	Form B	Form A

Because the comparison is between forms and not occasion, alternate forms reliability is not a coefficient of stability. Rather, it is a *coefficient of equivalence*. The primary source of error is test forms, but other sources of error, such as fatigue and learning, are also at play. The coefficient reflects the extent to which test forms are interchangeable. When test forms are very similar and observed scores are not adversely impacted by test form-specific content or difficulty, the alternate forms reliability coefficient will be high. Conversely, as the composition and difficulty between the two forms diverge, the estimate will decrease.

Alternate forms reliability reduces the influence of practice effects, but the influence of fatigue remains. As such, the time interval between administrations still must be given careful consideration. It must be long enough to minimize the influence of fatigue. An additional challenge in using the alternate forms approach is the development of two test forms. In some situations, the creation of two test forms may be cost prohibitive.

Test-Retest with Alternate Forms. Features of the previous two designs are combined in the test-retest with alternate forms design. The purpose of this design is to reduce the impact of practice effects that are common to the test-retest method. Like the alternate forms method, examinees take a different form of the test on each of two occasions. Like the test-retest method, test forms are not counterbalanced, and the time interval between occasions should be several weeks. In this design, scores on the two forms are compared. The design is sensitive to error scores that result from variation of the characteristic being measured, as well as to differences in test form composition. It requires careful consideration of the time interval between occasions and the composition of each test form.

For example, suppose that all examinees took Form A of the ELA Benchmark and three months later took Form B (see Table 2.4). ELA is a characteristic that is likely to change quite a bit over several months, considering that students will continue to receive ELA instruction during that time. Moreover, there are some obvious differences in the content of the two test forms. See the percentage of items on each form for Reading 3 and Research 2 that are listed in Table 2.1. Both sources of error will

Table 2.4

Data Collection Design for Test-Retest with Alternate Forms

Person	Occasion 1	Occasion 2
P1	Form A	Form B
P2	Form A	Form B
P3	Form A	Form B
P4	Form A	Form B

affect the correlation of scores obtained from the two occasions. A shorter time interval, preferably one that does not involve additional ELA instruction, and test forms that are more similar would result in a larger reliability estimate in this situation. However, this larger reliability is no more correct than one obtained using a long time interval and dissimilar content. They are both correct, but each estimate should be interpreted with respect to the time interval and test form composition.

The benefit of using this method in lieu of the test-retest method depends on the amount of error contributed by differences in test forms relative to those introduced by practice effects. If practice effects are likely to contribute more error than test forms, the test-retest method with alternate forms is preferred. Conversely, if error due to test forms is likely to be greater than that due to practice effects, the test-retest method is preferred.

Estimating reliability through two whole-test replications is costly and time consuming. Test developers must cover the expense of two different test administrations and, if alternate forms are required, the expense of two different test forms. Examinees must spend twice the amount of time in testing simply to obtain an estimate of reliability. With two whole-test replications, the reliability estimate pertains to scores on one replication or the other, not the average score from both replications. Therefore, only one replication is actually needed for score reporting. The inefficiency of two whole-test replications is overcome by a single administration and subsequent partition of the test into two or more part-test replications.

Two Part-Test Replications

Many of the data collection designs commonly encountered in practical applications of classical test theory are based on part-test replications, in which a part-test may be considered half of a test, some other portion of the test items, or even a single test item. Table 2.5 generically depicts the data collection design for a part-test. In this design, data are collected on a single occasion by the administration of an entire test. However, the test is divided into parts for the computation of the reliability coefficient. The part-tests are referred to as items in Table 2.5, but the part tests need not be individual items. Each part-test may be considered a group of items. This section considers designs with two part-test replications (i.e., $n = 2$, Item 1 = part one, Item 2 = part two, and items 3 and 4 are ignored in Table 2.5).

Split-halves. The most basic way to estimate reliability from a single test administration is to divide the test into two halves, correlate the half-test scores, and adjust the correlation. Three methods for splitting a test in half are recommended: (a) randomly select half of the items to create one half-test form and assign the remaining items to the other half-test form, (b) create matched item pairs by selecting pairs of items with similar means and item-total correlations, and randomly assign an item from each pair to a form, and (c) assign the odd numbered items to one half and the even numbered items to another. Once two halves are established, the half-test scores may be correlated to obtain an estimate of half-test reliability. This reliability coefficient may be adjusted to full-length reliability using one of a variety of methods, each of

Table 2.5 **Data Collection Design for p x I**		
Person	**Occasion 1**	**Occasion 2**
P1	Item 1, Item 2, Item 3 Item 4	–
P2	Item 1, Item 2, Item 3 Item 4	–
P3	Item 1, Item 2, Item 3 Item 4	–
P4	Item 1, Item 2, Item 3 Item 4	–
Note: $n'_i = 4, n'_o = 1$		

which are discussed in Chapter 4 . The particular choice of adjustment method depends on the tenability of the assumptions underlying the part-test replications.

Other Two-part Divisions. Partitioning a test into two halves or two halves that contain similar content is not always possible. A test involving one or more testlets is an example. In test construction, testlets are often treated as a single question, and an entire testlet is assigned to a test form rather than individual items. Testlets may prevent one from splitting a test exactly in half, if each testlet contains a different number of items. One part of a test may contain many more items than another simply because of the presence of testlets in one or both part-test forms.

Dividing a test into two parts of equal length may also be difficult when one is interested in balancing the content of the two part-tests. Depending on the order of the items and the content area measured by each item, an odd-even split may result in two part-tests that measure different aspects of a test's table of specifications. For example, an odd-even split of the benchmark ELA test results in two part-tests that differentially represent the test's content areas (see Table 2.6). Notice the different percentages of items tapping into each content area and the manner in which these percentages differ between the odd and even part-tests. In particular, notice that only the odd half contains items that measure Research 1. If the two part-tests were modified

Table 2.6

Odd-Even Partition of Test: Number and Percentage (in Parentheses) of Items in Each ELA Content Areas

Content Area	Odd Half	Even Half
Reading 1	11 (34)	11 (34)
Reading 2	13 (41)	11 (34)
Reading 3	5 (16)	8 (25)
Research 1	2 (6)	0 (0)
Research 2	1 (3)	2 (6)
Total	32 (100)	32 (100)

Table 2.7 Content Partition of Test: Number and Percentage (in Parentheses) of Items in Each ELA Content Areas		
Content Area	Part 1	Part 2
Reading 1	11 (36)	11 (33)
Reading 2	12 (39)	12 (36)
Reading 3	6 (19)	7 (21)
Research 1	1 (3)	1 (3)
Research 2	1 (3)	2 (6)
Total	31 (100)	33 (100)

to better balance the five content areas, the two part-tests may no longer be equal in length. For example, Table 2.7 lists another way to assign items to the part tests in order to better balance content. The resulting two part-tests no longer have the same number of items, although the difference is only two items. This unequal test length may seem innocuous, but, as explained in the next chapter, it has implications for the assumptions underlying the nature of each replication and the selection of a reliability estimator. The ELA example demonstrates that balancing content between two part-tests of equal length can be difficult, particularly if testlets are present.

There are many ways to divide a test into two parts of equal length, and additional ways to divide a test into two parts of unequal length. The difficulty in selecting a two-part division of a test is a limitation of this approach. Suppose a test consists of $n = n_1 + n_2$ items, of which n_1 items will be assigned to one part-test and the remaining n_2 items will be assigned to the other part-test. There are $\frac{1}{2} \left[\frac{(n_1+n_2)!}{n_1!n_2!} \right]$ unique ways to split a test into two halves (i.e., $n_1 = n_2$)[1], and $\left[\frac{(n_1+n_2)!}{n_1!n_2!} \right]$ unique ways to divide the test into two unique parts of unequal length (i.e., $n_1 \neq n_2$). For

---

[1] The symbol "!" denotes the factorial function. For example, 4! is read "four factorial," and it equals $4 \times 3 \times 2 \times 1 = 24$.

example, a 20-item test may be split into $\frac{20!}{10!10!} \frac{1}{2} = 92{,}378$ unique half-tests. If there is reason to assign five items to one part-test and 15 items to the other part-test, there are $\frac{20!}{5!15!} = 15{,}504$ possible ways to achieve such a partition of the test items. Given the number of possibilities, it should be clear that there is no one "true" partition of the items. Any partition of the items into two parts is defensible, and each partition will likely result in a different estimate of reliability. The number of possibilities for partitioning a test into two parts is a limitation of this method.

Multiple Part-test Divisions. Dividing a test into two parts is not always suitable. If a test is comprised entirely of testlets like the eighth grade ELA Benchmark assessment, it makes more sense to treat each testlet as a separate part, rather than arbitrarily partition the test into two parts (Feldt, 2002). This approach would divide the ELA Benchmark test into eight parts—one part for each testlet.

Testlets are not the only reason to divide a test into multiple parts. In many applications, a test may contain multiple item types such as multiple-choice, short-answer, and extended-response items. In these situations, it is more appropriate to have each part represent an item type (Qualls, 1995). For example, all of the multiple-choice items would form one part. The short-answer would form another part. A third part would be comprised of the extended-response items.

There are many ways to partition a test into multiple parts. One may be to balance the test specifications, whereas another may be to balance test specifications and item type. The number of all possible k part-test partitions is given by the multinomial coefficient, $\frac{(n_1 + n_2 + \cdots + n_k)!}{n_1! n_2! \ldots n_k!}$. To demonstrate this computation, a 20-item test can be divided into four parts of equal length in $\frac{20!}{5!5!5!5!} = 11{,}732{,}745{,}024$ ways. Each possible partition will result in a different reliability estimate. Like the two-part test partitions, the multiple part-test division makes it difficult to determine which partition is most appropriate. Some may be justified on logical or test construction grounds, but all are "correct."

The most common applications of multiple part-test partitions treat each item as a part. Well-known coefficients such as Cronbach's α (Cronbach, 1951), Raju's β (Raju, 1977), and Guttman's λ (Guttman, 1945) are three examples. An additional benefit of these estimates is that they solve the problem of determining which partition of the test to use. These estimates result in the average value for all possible half-test replications without having to compute the reliability estimate for all possible partitions (Cronbach). Deciding whether to use, for example, Cronbach's α or Guttman's λ is a matter of the assumptions one is willing to make about the test scores. This decision process is discussed in Chapter 4.

Whether one is splitting a test in two or dividing the test into 10 parts, all of the possible partitions reflect only one source of measurement error: error due to the sampling of items. As such, estimates that use part-test replications are referred to as *internal consistency* estimates. They reflect relationships among items. Other sources of error, such as occasion, are not explicitly part of these coefficients. Multiple sources of error can be included in the data collection design using generalizability theory, as will be discussed shortly.

Data Collection Designs for Classification Decisions

Data collection designs for classification decisions are similar to whole-test replications described for classical test theory. A design involves either one or two whole-test replications. One major difference is that a cut-score is included in each replication for measures that involve classification decisions. Hence, a cut-score and the process of standard setting itself may be considered part of the data collection design. Altering the cut-score changes the definition and interpretation of reliability for classification decisions. Indeed, reliability for classification decisions may be improved by simply increasing or decreasing the cut-score. Collecting data for classification decisions requires observation of one or two measurement procedures and the establishment of one or more cut-scores. The design remains a two-factor design and is thus limited to one source of error.

Data Collection Designs in Generalizability Theory

Generalizability theory builds on the factorial nature of data collection designs and permits multiple sources of error to be analyzed simultaneously. Moreover, the design may involve facets[2] that are fully crossed, fully nested, or partially nested. This flexibility results in a single framework that can account for a seemingly endless number of data collection designs. The challenge is limiting the possibilities to one or more designs that are most appropriate for a given situation.

There are two purposes for conducting a decision study, and each one provides guidance on selecting a data collection design. A measurement procedure that is well established is not likely to undergo revisions prior to the next administration. Therefore, a data collection design that matches the observed design is the only one of interest. The purpose of a decision study in this scenario is to estimate reliability for the observed measurement procedure.

Conversely, a measurement procedure in development will likely be modified before the next administration. Therefore, any data collection design that improves the efficiency and reliability of a measurement procedure is of interest. Eligible designs are not limited to the observed design. (Recall that the observed design pertains to the measurement procedure actually implemented to collected data for the generalizability study. The data collection design is part of the decision study, and it may or may not be the same as the observed design.) In this scenario, the purpose of a decision study is to estimate reliability for a variety of designs and select one that best refines the measurement procedure. Future observed designs are then based on the refined procedure.

Each data collection design affects the definition of universe score, universe score variance, and error variance. As a result, each design results in a different estimate and interpretation of reliability; the numerator and denominator in Equation 1.28 and Equation 1.29 may differ with each design. Given the plethora of data collection designs, this section will only discuss designs that (a) are commonly encountered in research, (b) make connections

---

[2] Notice the difference in language. *Factors* refer to everything in the design, but *facets* refer to factors that are sources of measurement error. The *object of measurement* refers to the examinee factor. Therefore, a two-factor design in the experimental literature is the same as a one-facet design in generalizability theory. The number of factors in generalizability theory is the object of measurement plus the number of facets.

between classical test theory and generalizability theory, and (c) are specific to the ELA Benchmark assessment.

Common Data Collection Designs

Random Designs. The most basic design in generalizability theory is the $p \times I$ design (see Table 2.5). It is a design typically used in classical test theory, and it leads to some of the same reliability estimates. Unlike classical test theory, analysis of this design in generalizability theory results in estimates of three different sources of variance: p, I, and pI. Each of these sources of variance may be combined in different ways—according to the type of decision of interest (i.e., relative or absolute)—to produce an estimate of reliability.

A slightly more complex design, but one that still only permits one source of measurement error, is the $I : p$ design. As shown in Table 2.8, each examinee is administered a different set of items, but all items are administered on the same occasion. An example of this design is computerized adaptive testing (CAT; van der Linden & Glass, 2000). A CAT is composed of items tailored to each individual examinee, as determined by a computer algorithm. As such, each examinee may be given a different set of items. There are only two sources of variance in this design: p, and $I{:}p$. As a result, expressions for relative and absolute error are the same in this design.

Two sources of measurement error and their interactions are captured in a two-facet $p \times I \times O$ design (see Table 2.9). In this design, items and occasions are the two facets. The facets and the

Table 2.8 **Data Collection Design for I:p**		
Person	**Occasion 1**	**Occasion 2**
P1	Item 1, Item 2	–
P2	Item 3, Item 4	–
P3	Item 5, Item 6	–
P4	Item 7, Item 8	–
Note: $n'_i = 2, n'_o = 1$		

Table 2.9
Data Collection Design for p x I x O

Person	Occasion 1	Occasion 2
P1	Item 1, Item 2	Item 1, Item 2
P2	Item 1, Item 2	Item 1, Item 2
P3	Item 1, Item 2	Item 1, Item 2
P4	Item 1, Item 2	Item 1, Item 2

Note: $n'_i = 2, n'_o = 2$

object of measurement (i.e., persons) are fully crossed. Data collection involves administering the same items to every examinee on every occasion. This design partitions the total variability into seven different sources: p, I, O, pI, pO, IO, and pIO. Reliability estimates from this design (and other data collection designs) pertain to examinees scores that are averaged over all facets. In the $p \times I \times O$ design, an examinee's individual scores (i.e., scores for each item on each occasion) are averaged over items and occasions.

In some measurement applications, examinees are administered a different test form on different occasions. The SC Benchmark test is a good example. Given that each occasion involves a different set of items, the items are nested within occasion. Table 2.10 demonstrates the data collection design when

Table 2.10
Data Collection Design for $p \times (I{:}O)$

Person	Occasion 1	Occasion 2
P1	Item 1, Item 2	Item 3, Item 4
P2	Item 1, Item 2	Item 3, Item 4
P3	Item 1, Item 2	Item 3, Item 4
P4	Item 1, Item 2	Item 3, Item 4

Note: $n'_i = 2, n'_o = 2$

items are nested within occasion. Total observed score variance is partitioned into five sources: p, O, $I{:}O$, pO, and $pI{:}O$.

Mixed Designs. A data collection design not only involves a definition of the number of facets and the organization of facets (i.e., crossed or nested), but also a specification of the size of the universe of generalization. A design may involve all random (i.e., infinite) facets, or a combination of random and fixed facets. The former design is referred to as a *random effects design*, whereas the latter is called a *mixed design*. The only restriction is that a design must have at least one random facet. Therefore, a single-facet design always involves a random facet. A two-facet design, however, may have one random and one fixed facet. As explained in detail shortly, fixing a facet can affect the definition of a universe score and increase universe score variance. The result is that reliability estimates tend to be higher for a mixed design than a random design with the same facet sample sizes and organization of facets.

Mixed designs involve at least one fixed facet. Deciding which (if any) facet to fix depends on the definition of a measurement procedure replication. A facet should be fixed if all levels of the facet are observed in a measurement procedure. That is, the observed procedure exhausts all levels of a facet. For example, a design with a fixed items facet assumes that the items included in the measurement procedure exhaust all items in the universe. No other items exist or will be developed for the measurement procedure. Fixing a facet potentially increases universe score variance and reduces error variance thereby increasing estimates of reliability. It also redefines the universe score and limits the universe of generalization. Therefore, reliability estimates from mixed designs necessarily have an interpretation different from those from random designs. Generalizations beyond the fixed facet are not permissible.

Fixing an effect has the potential to increase the value of universe score variance while decreasing relative and absolute error variance. Consider the variance terms for the $p \times I \times O$ and $p \times (I : O)$ designs. Fixing occasions in either design changes the expressions for universe score variance and error variance. This result is evident by comparing expressions in Tables 1.2 and 2.11. Notice that the person-by-occasion interaction component is

Table 2.11

Universe Score, Relative Error, and Absolute Error Variance for Mixed Designs (Items Random, Occasions Fixed)

Design	Variance	Expression
$p \times I \times O$	Universe Score	$\sigma^2(p) = \sigma^2(p) + \dfrac{\sigma^2(po)}{n'_o}$
	Relative Error	$\sigma^2(\delta) = \dfrac{\sigma^2(pi)}{n'_i} + \dfrac{\sigma^2(pio)}{n'_i n'_o}$
	Absolute Error	$\sigma^2(\Delta) = \dfrac{\sigma^2(i)}{n'_i} + \dfrac{\sigma^2(pi)}{n'_i} + \dfrac{\sigma^2(io)}{n'_i n'_o} + \dfrac{\sigma^2(pio)}{n'_i n'_o}$
$p \times (I : O)$	Universe Score	$\sigma^2(p) = \sigma^2(p) + \dfrac{\sigma^2(po)}{n'_o}$
	Relative Error	$\sigma^2(\delta) = \dfrac{\sigma^2(pi : o)}{n'_i n'_o}$
	Absolute Error	$\sigma^2(\Delta) = \dfrac{\sigma^2(i : o)}{n'_i n'_o} + \dfrac{\sigma^2(pi : o)}{n'_i n'_o}$

added to universe score variance and removed from error variance. The variance component for occasions is also removed from absolute error variance. Consequently, generalizability and Φ coefficient estimates based on components from a mixed design potentially involve a larger numerator and smaller denominator than corresponding estimates from a random design. Subsequently, a mixed design reliability estimate may be larger than a random design estimate, given the same facet sample sizes.

Fixing a facet does not always increase universe score variance and decrease error variance. The result depends on the design and which facet is fixed. Fixing the item facet changes the expression for universe score variance and error variance in the $p \times I \times O$ design, but not the $p \times (I : O)$ design (details not shown). Universe score and error variance are the same for the random $p \times (I : O)$ design and the mixed design with items fixed. This result makes sense conceptually. If the occasion facet is random (i.e., infinite) and items are nested within occasion, then items are necessarily random. Therefore, the $p \times (I : O)$ design with items fixed has the same variance components as the $p \times (I : O)$ with items random.

Although a data collection design may differ from the observed design, there are some limitations. A facet that is nested in the observed design (i.e., the generalizability study) may not be crossed in the data collection design (i.e., the decision study), and a facet that is fixed in an observed design may not be random in a data collection design. Therefore, the greatest number of data collection design possibilities occurs when the observed design is fully crossed and random.

Classical Test Theory Designs Restated as Data Collection Designs

The test-retest, test-retest with alternate forms, and multi-part division designs in classical test theory may also be characterized in generalizability theory by data collection designs that involve a hidden facet. A *hidden facet* results when a facet has a sample size of 1, causing the facet variance components to be confounded with variance components for other facets. Hidden facets are not evident in classical test theory designs. However, restating these designs as data collection designs in generalizability theory obviates the hidden facet. The test-retest design described in Table 2.2 is based on a $p \times I \times O$ data collection design in generalizability theory, but the number of occasions in the data collection design differ from the number of occasions in the observed design. Brennan (2001b) explains that the test-retest design allows one to estimate reliability for scores from one test occasion or the other, not the average of scores from the two occasions. Specifically, the test-retest design is equivalent to a $p \times I \times O$ data collection design with a fixed-item facet and a random occasion facet with one occasion (i.e., $n'_o = 1$). The occasion facet is considered to be random because it makes no difference if reliability pertains to scores from the first or second occasion. If one were interested in assigning scores that were the average of the two occasions, then the appropriate data collection design would have two occasions (i.e., $n'_o = 2$). In this latter design, error variance due to occasion and interactions with occasion would be smaller, and the subsequent reliability estimate would be larger, because the facet sample size is larger. However, the interpretation of a reliability estimate resulting from this latter design differs from the interpretation of an estimate from a test-retest design; the estimate either pertains to scores from a single occasion or scores averaged over occasions.

Brennan (2001b) also described a data collection design for the test-retest with alternate forms design listed in Table 2.4. The test-retest with alternate forms design also produces a reliability estimate that pertains to scores from one occasion only, not the average of scores from both occasions. Therefore, the number of occasions is 1. Items are nested within occasion in the test-retest with alternate forms design because a different test form (i.e., a different group of items) is administered on each occasion. This design is denoted $p \times (I : O)$. Like the test-retest design, the occasion facet is random in the test-retest with alternate forms design. This facet is random because it makes no difference which form is selected for the first occasion and which is selected for the second. Unlike the test-retest design, items are also random. The reason items are random is that a design with an infinite (i.e., random) number of occasions, each with a unique set of items, implies that items are also infinite. This consideration helps explain why a $p \times (I : O)$ design with items fixed and occasions random results in the same variance components as the same design with items random and occasions random.

Finally, the multi-part division design (i.e., designs for internal consistency) may be conceptualized as data collection designs in two ways. The first is a $p \times I$ design with items random (see Table 2.5). If the number of items in the data collection design is the same as the number of items in observed design, and the error term describes relative error, the resulting generalizability coefficient (Equation 1.28) is equivalent to Cronbach's α. However, Brennan (2001a) argued that a multi-part division design entails a hidden occasion facet. Therefore, the data collection design is actually a $p \times I \times O$ design with one occasion, a fixed occasion facet, and a random item facet.

Data Collection Designs for the ELA Benchmark Assessment

Table 2.12 lists several possible data collection designs, given the ELA Benchmark generalizability study. This list is by no means

Table 2.12
Possible Data Collection Designs for the ELA Benchmarks with Items Random

Design	Purpose	Items (n'_i)	Occasions (n'_o)	Occasions
1	Observed Design	32	2	Random
2	Reduce Items	28	2	Random
3	Reduce Items	24	2	Random
4	Reduce Items	32	2	Fixed
5	Reduce Items	28	2	Fixed
6	Reduce Items	24	2	Fixed
7	Reduce Occasions	64	1	Random
8	Reduce Occasions and Items	56	1	Random
9	Reduce Occasions and Items	48	1	Random
10	Reduce Occasions	64	1	Fixed
11	Reduce Occasions and Items	56	1	Fixed
12	Reduce Occasions and Items	48	1	Fixed

exhaustive, but it illustrates several data collection designs that serve different purposes. Only the first row of Table 2.12 corresponds to the actual way in which data were collected for the generalizability study (i.e., the observed design). The additional rows describe more efficient alternative designs that involve fewer items within a testlet, fewer occasions, or both. The impact of such efficiencies on the measurement procedure is evaluated by considering a variety of designs in a decision study. An argument could then be made for using a more efficient design, if reliability tends to be comparable to the less efficient observed design.

Measurement procedure efficiencies are not the only reason one would consider alternative data collection designs. If an observed design resulted in low reliability, one would seek ways to improve it. Facets sample sizes may be increased to evaluate the impact on reliability. For example, the number of items within an occasion may be increased from 32 to 50. Similarly, the number of occasions could be increased. The most efficient way to increase reliability is to focus on the largest variance components and increase the sample sizes for the facet or facets involving those components.

Chapter Summary

This chapter related data collection designs to within-subjects factorial designs. In classical test theory and classification decisions, data collection designs are two-factor designs. One factor represents examinees, and the other a source of measurement error. The source of error may vary, but each design is a two-factor design.

Generalizability theory builds on the factorial nature of data collection designs and permits one or more facets to be included in the design. The facets may be crossed, nested, or partially nested; a strength of generalizability theory identified by Cronbach (Cronbach & Shavelson, 2004). In addition, facets may be fixed or random, as long as the design includes at least one random facet.

Data collection designs contribute to the definition of a measurement procedure replication. However, to fully define a replication and identify an appropriate reliability coefficient, the assumptions underlying each replication must be established. The next chapter describes assumptions in detail, along with the consequences for violating them. Once the data collection design and underlying assumptions have been established, a reliability coefficient may be selected. Chapter 4 describes a variety of coefficients that are likely to be used in an analysis.

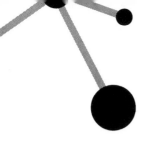

3

ASSUMPTIONS

ASSUMPTIONS ABOUT a measurement procedure and the nature of test scores fall into three different categories: assumptions about (a) dimensionality, (c) error score correlations, and (c) the nature of measurement procedure replications. Assumptions in these categories, in conjunction with the data collection design and item type, guide the selection of an appropriate reliability coefficient. In this chapter, each type of assumption is described in detail, followed by a discussion of the consequences for violating the assumption. This information sets the stage for selecting an appropriate method for estimating reliability, as discussed in the next chapter.

Dimensionality

Dimensionality refers to the number of factors or dimensions underlying scores produced from a measurement procedure. For example, the Benchmark assessment of English Language Arts (ELA) measures a single factor, English Language Arts, whereas the Achievement Goal Questionnaire (Elliot & McGregor, 2001) measures four factors, Performance Approach, Mastery Avoidance, Mastery Approach, and Performance Avoidance. The desired number of dimensions is determined by the theoretical basis of the construct. However, theory does not guarantee that a measurement procedure will tap into the desired number of dimensions. Dimensionality must be empirically tested upon each observation of the measurement procedure.

A variety of terms are commonly encountered in the literature on dimensionality, but these terms are not used in a standard way. Some authors (e.g. Kline, 1998) use the term *unidimensional* to describe a measurement procedure in which items correspond to one and only one factor, but the measure may involve one or more factors. Those authors use the term *multidimensional* to refer to cases in which the measure involves multiple factors, and items contribute to two or more factors. To clarify the language, this text will refer to the former case as *simple structure* and the latter as *complex structure*. Moreover, a measurement procedure that involves only one factor is referred to as *unidimensional*, and a measurement procedure that involves two or more factors is referred to as *multidimensional*. A multidimensional measure may involve simple or complex structures. Synonyms for unidimensional and multidimensional measures commonly encountered in the literature are *homogenous* and *heterogeneous* tests, respectively. With this clarification of terminology, the necessary assumption about dimensionality may be stated.

All methods for estimating reliability discussed in this text assume that the measurement procedure is unidimensional. There is only one true score, T, for an examinee in classical test theory (see Equation 1.1); only one domain score distribution (see Equation 1.6) for an examinee in strong true score theory; and only one universe score, v_p, for an examinee in generalizability theory (see Equation 1.22). The assumption of unidimensionality is critical to selecting an appropriate method for estimating reliability. This assumption is tested first, and it should be tested prior to selecting a method for estimating reliability (Komaroff, 1997; Osburn, 2000; Raykov, 1998, 2001). Ironically, most researchers do not learn how to test unidimensionality until after learning about reliability. Methods for testing unidimensionality are complex and only encountered in statistics classes that are more advanced than courses on score reliability. Therefore, these methods are only briefly described here.

Selecting a method to test unidimensionality depends on the nature and amount of data. When data are presumed to be normally distributed, unidimensionality may be evaluated using exploratory or confirmatory factor analysis (see Kline, 1998; Stevens, 1996). One such method is described by Raykov (1997). Other methods such as DIMTEST (Stout, 1987) are available for evaluating the assumption of unidimensionality with non-normally distributed data, such as binary items (i.e., items scored right or wrong). Dimensionality should only be tested by these methods when the sample size is adequate (Raykov, 2001). Unfortunately, most methods for testing dimensionality require a large sample size (see Finch & Habing, 2007; Gagné & Hancock, 2006).

For a small sample size, few options exist for testing dimensionality. Dimensionality may be explored by checking the inter-item correlations for patterns of low or negative correlations (Green, Lissitz, & Mulaik, 1977). This information, combined with the theoretical basis for a construct, may provide some evidence in support of unidimensionality, but a formal confirmatory test is preferred.

Cronbach's α and other measures of internal consistency are not tests of unidimensionality (Cronbach, 1951; Schmitt, 1996). Internal consistency refers to the interrelatedness of items, but unidimensionality means that only one factor underlies test scores. Internal consistency is required for unidimensionality, but it does not guarantee unidimensionality (Cortina, 1993; Cronbach, 1951; Green et al., 1977; Schmitt, 1996). Internal consistency may be high even when a test measures multiple dimensions. This result occurs when common factors account for a large portion of test variance (Cronbach, 1951). Several authors have demonstrated that high values of Cronbach's α may be observed with multidimensional scores (Cortina, 1993; Feldt & Qualls, 1996; Green et al., 1977; Osburn, 2000; Schmitt, 1996). Therefore, Cronbach's α and other measures of internal consistency should never be used as a measure of unidimensionality.

Violation of Unidimensionality

Reliability is underestimated when scores are not unidimensional (Cortina, 1993; Cronbach, 1951; Feldt & Qualls, 1996; Osburn, 2000). The estimate may still be reasonably high, but it will be smaller than it should be. For example, Osburn demonstrated that with a true reliability value of 0.76, Cronbach's α was only 0.7 when scores were multidimensional. This difference may seem small, but there is no guarantee that it will always be so small. It is better to avoid the influence of multidimensionality altogether by ensuring that scores are unidimensional or using a method of estimating reliability that is appropriate for multidimensional measures.

Stratified α is a method for estimating reliability for multi-dimensional scores that have simple structure (Cronbach, Schönemann, & McKie, 1965; Rajaratnam, Cronbach, & Gleser, 1965). It works by dividing the content areas, subscales, or factors of a multidimensional measure into separate strata, and then pooling the within-strata error variances. It increases (or decreases) as the pooled within-strata error variance decreases (or increases). Stratified α diverges the most from Cronbach's α for multidimensional measures with simple structure and uncorrelated factors (Cronbach et al., 1965). In this situation, stratified α will be higher than Cronbach's α and closer to the true value. As the magnitude of the correlations between strata approaches the magnitude of inter-item correlations within strata, Cronbach's α will approach the value of stratified α (Cronbach et al.; Rajaratnam et al., 1965).

If test scores are multidimensional and multiple sources of error are present, *multivariate generalizability theory* provides the best way to estimate reliability. Indeed, stratified α was developed in the context of multivariate generalizability theory (Brennan, 2001b). This method is beyond the scope of this text, but the reader is encouraged to read Brennan's text on generalizability theory for more information.

Error Score Correlations

Error scores were described in Chapter 1 and denoted by an E in Equation 1.1. The notion of error score correlations is related closely to dimensionality. Error score correlations may represent shared sources of variance other than those due to a common factor (Kline, 1998). In this situation, only a subset of items may show error score correlations. A more extreme case arises when correlated errors are due to use of a model that specifies fewer dimensions than it should. In this situation, all items will exhibit error score correlations (Raykov, 1998). The following assumption about error score correlations simplifies the development of many reliability coefficients, but violation of this assumption may result in biased estimates.

All methods for estimating reliability discussed in this text assume that error scores are uncorrelated. This assumption was specifically stated for classical test theory but it also pertains to classification decisions and generalizability theory.

Violation of Uncorrelated Errors

A variety of authors have demonstrated that internal consistency estimates of reliability are artificially inflated in the presence of positively correlated errors (Green & Hershberger, 2000; Komaroff, 1997; Lucke, 2005; Raykov, 1998, 2001; Zimmerman & Williams, 1980; Zimmerman, Zumbo, & LaLonde, 1993). However, this effect is not consistent; it is confounded by the effect of violating other assumptions. If errors are correlated because of an unspecified underlying factor, internal consistency will be underestimated (Green & Hershberger). Moreover, if the assumptions of unidimensionality, τ-equivalence (described later), and correlated errors are simultaneously violated, the effect on estimates of internal consistency is less predictable. Komaroff (1997) and Raykov (1998) indicate that the negative bias of multidimensionality is not only attenuated by the positive bias of correlated errors, but that the positive bias may prevail, thus resulting in an overestimate of reliability. Given the variety of ways that correlated errors may influence measures of internal consistency, the assumption should be examined through consideration of possible sources of correlated error that may occur in a measurement procedure. Statistical methods may then be selected to best account for these violations.

Correlated errors may be caused by a variety of things likely to be encountered in normal testing practice, such as test speededness, testlets, context effects, and model misspecification (Lucke, 2005; Raykov, 2001). *Test speededness* refers to the situation in which some examinees are unable to complete a test within the time limit. These examinees either leave the unreached items as unanswered or rapidly guesses the response to remaining items to complete the test within the time limit. In either case, item responses are predominantly incorrect. A split-half reliability estimate computed from a first-half/second-half split, will underestimate reliability (Traub, 1994). Conversely, if the coefficient is based on an odd-even split, the reliability estimate will be larger than it should be (Traub). The latter effect is a result of a perfect correlation among unreached items in each half that are scored incorrect or the qualitatively different response patterns among rapidly guessed items.

Testlets are groups of related items. The Benchmark assessment of ELA is an example. Each testlet involves eight questions that involve a single reading prompt. A group of math items that share a graph is another example. The problem of correlated error occurs in testlets because within-testlet item correlations tend to be larger than the between-testlet item correlations. Conditions of testing may also result in correlated errors.

Context effects are conditions of the testing that persistently influence scores. Item placement and order effects are examples. The occasion of testing is another. Context effects that arise due to test occasion may affect the relationship among items. For example, a test administered on a Thursday and Friday is likely to show an occasion effect. Students may put forth effort and aspire to obtain the correct response on Thursday, but on Friday students may be distracted by the coming weekend and exhibit a tendency to provide incorrect responses. As a result, test occasion may induce a correlation among items if it is not specifically treated as part of a model (i.e., when it is a hidden facet).

Finally, *model misspecification* occurs when an important feature of the data is not included in a model. A measurement model that involves fewer factors than it should is an example. As explained previously, fitting a unidimensional model to multidimensional data will cause correlated errors among items. Hidden facets are another example of a way in which model misspecification may result in correlated errors.

Most methods for testing the assumption of uncorrelated error are complex and beyond the scope of this text. Exploratory and confirmatory factor analysis, structural equation modeling, and item-response theory provide techniques for testing this assumption and estimating reliability. Raykov (1998), Komaroff (1997), and Green and Hershberger (2000) describe factor analytic and structural equation modeling methods for handling correlated error. Mixture item response theory models (Rost, 1990) or the testlet model (Wainer, Bradlow, & Wang, 2007) are viable alternatives that do not assume normally distributed item responses. Perhaps the simplest alternative is to include the source of correlated error in a data collection design and estimate reliability using generalizability theory. For example, a testlet may be included in a data collection design by treating items as nested within a testlet. Context effects and the influence of the test occasion may be included in the model in a similar fashion.

Assumptions related to dimensionality and error score correlations are commonly overlooked in practical applications of test score reliability. However, violating these assumptions may notably bias the reliability estimate. These assumptions must be considered along with the more well-known assumptions in measurement that are described in the next section.

The Nature of Measurement Procedure Replications

Classical Test Theory

In Chapter 1, replications in classical test theory were described in terms of the defining characteristics of the theory, and many of those features are tautologies. They are true by definition, and we cannot test the veracity of such claims. However, there are also testable assumptions that further define classical test theory and the nature of replications. The assumptions of unidimensionality and uncorrelated errors are two such assumptions. Feldt and Brennan (1989) described additional assumptions about the nature of measurement procedure replications, which they referred to as the *degree of part-test similarity*. These assumptions are listed below in order from the least restrictive to most restrictive to demonstrate the nested structure of the assumptions. That is, a more restrictive assumption is defined by constraining parameters on a less restrictive assumption. This nested structure has important implications for conducting formal statistical tests of the assumptions (see Jöreskog, 1971; Reuterberg & Gustafsson, 1992). Example covariance matrices based on those described in Feldt (2002) are provided to illuminate the consequences of each assumption and emphasize their nested organization. These matrices are based on four part-test replications, but they may be easily extended to describe measures composed of more parts.

Congeneric Measures. The assumption of congeneric measures (Jöreskog, 1971) is the youngest and most general. All other assumptions in classical test theory (i.e., τ-equivalence, essential τ-equivalence, and parallel) are nested within congeneric measures and may be obtained through certain restrictions on the congeneric assumption.

A pair of replications (e.g., test items, part-tests) are congeneric if they have unequal error variances, and the true score for person i on one replication is a linear transformation of the true score from a second replication. This implies that congeneric measures have (a) different expected (i.e., average) observed scores, (b) different true score variances, (c) different observed score variances, (d) different covariance and correlations between observed scores from any pair of congeneric measures, (e) different covariance and correlations for any congeneric measure and an external measure, and (f) different reliabilities.

To further understand the implications of congeneric measures, consider either $j = 1, \ldots, k$ whole-test replications or a single n item test divided into k part-test replications (e.g., each item represents a part, $n = k$). The k components involved in either case will be referred to as "parts." As described in Feldt (2002), the observed score for examinee a on part j is the proportional contribution of the part to the total true score, $\lambda_j T_a$, plus person-specific error, E_{aj}, plus a constant, c_j. Specifically,

$$X_{aj} = \lambda_j T_a + E_{aj} + c_j. \tag{3.1}$$

The *effective test length* parameter[1] λ_j reflects each part's proportional contribution to the composite true score and, subsequently, each part's contribution to the total true score variance. It may or may not be proportional to the size (i.e., number of items on) of

---

[1] In factor analysis, the effective test length parameter is referred to as a factor loading. The effective test length parameters are factor loadings constrained to be nonzero proportions that sum to unity. Total true score variance (i.e. factor variance) is unconstrained and freely estimated when effective test length parameters are used. In factor analysis, factor variance is constrained to unity while some factor loadings are unconstrained and freely estimated.

each part (Feldt). It is constrained, such that $\lambda_j > 0$ and $\sum_{j=1}^{k} \lambda_j = 1$. As a result, true scores on two congeneric measures are related by

$$T_{2a} = \frac{\lambda_1}{\lambda_2} T_{1a} + c_{12} \qquad (3.2)$$

where c_{12} is a constant equal to $(c_1 - c_2)/\lambda_2$. The constant indicates that true scores from one replication may be larger or smaller than true scores on another, and the effective length parameter allows true scores from the two replications to have a different scale, yet be perfectly correlated.

To explain the implications of Equation 3.1, consider a covariance matrix for a $k = 4$ part test:

$$\begin{pmatrix} \lambda_1^2 \sigma_T^2 + \sigma_{E_1}^2 & \lambda_1 \lambda_2 \sigma_T^2 & \lambda_1 \lambda_3 \sigma_T^2 & \lambda_1 \lambda_4 \sigma_T^2 \\ \lambda_2 \lambda_1 \sigma_T^2 & \lambda_2^2 \sigma_T^2 + \sigma_{E_2}^2 & \lambda_2 \lambda_3 \sigma_T^2 & \lambda_2 \lambda_4 \sigma_T^2 \\ \lambda_3 \lambda_1 \sigma_T^2 & \lambda_3 \lambda_2 \sigma_T^2 & \lambda_3^2 \sigma_T^2 + \sigma_{E_3}^2 & \lambda_3 \lambda_4 \sigma_T^2 \\ \lambda_4 \lambda_1 \sigma_T^2 & \lambda_4 \lambda_2 \sigma_T^2 & \lambda_4 \lambda_3 \sigma_T^2 & \lambda_4^2 \sigma_T^2 + \sigma_{E_4}^2 \end{pmatrix}, \qquad (3.3)$$

where σ_T^2 is the composite true score variance (i.e. factor variance). Observed score variance for the entire four-part composite is the sum of all elements of this matrix. It can be broken down into different components. The unique subscript on each error variance indicates that the error variance for each part is allowed to differ from any or all other error variances. Similarly, the unique subscript on each effective length parameter indicates that each part has a different loading on the composite true score and composite true score variance. Different combinations of true score and error score variances along the upper left to lower right diagonal indicate that each part can have a different observed score variance. For example, the observed score variance for part 1 is $\sigma_{X_1}^2 = \lambda_1^2 \sigma_T^2 + \sigma_{E_1}^2$. In addition to the unique aspects of each congeneric part, relationships among the parts are evident in Equation 3.3.

True scores for any two parts are perfectly correlated. For example, the true score correlation for part 1 and part 2 is

$$\frac{\lambda_1 \lambda_2 \sigma_T^2}{\sqrt{\lambda_1^2 \sigma_T^2} \sqrt{\lambda_2^2 \sigma_T^2}} = 1. \tag{3.4}$$

In contrast, the observed score covariance and correlation may differ for each pair of parts. Different combinations of effective length parameters for the off-diagonal elements indicate that the covariance between any pair of parts may differ from the covariance between any other pair of parts. The correlation between pairs may also differ. For example, the observed score correlation between parts 1 and 2 is

$$\rho_{12} = \frac{\lambda_1 \lambda_2 \sigma_T^2}{\sigma_{X_1} \sigma_{X_2}},$$

where $\sigma_{X_j} = \sqrt{\lambda_j^2 \sigma_T^2 + \sigma_{E_j}^2}$. Given that the numerator (i.e., the covariance) and denominator can differ for each pair of parts, the correlations for each pair can differ. Finally, reliability for each part can differ. For example, the reliability for part 1 is

$$\rho_{XT}^2 = \frac{\lambda_1^2 \sigma_T^2}{\lambda_1^2 \sigma_T^2 + \sigma_{E_1}^2}.$$

Each part may have different values in the numerator and denominator and, therefore, a different reliability.

Although the assumption of congeneric measures is arguably the most tenable in practice, estimating congeneric reliability coefficients is difficult and may require iterative procedures (see Jöreskog, 1971; Reuterberg & Gustafsson, 1992). An easier method for estimating reliability requires the assumption of classical congeneric measures, a slightly different assumption than congeneric.

Classical Congeneric Measures. Classical *congeneric* measures (Feldt, 1975, 2002; Feldt & Brennan, 1989) require that the contribution of each part to the composite error variance be proportional to the effective test length. The covariance matrix for classical congeneric measures with four parts is

$$
\begin{pmatrix}
\lambda_1^2 \sigma_T^2 + \lambda_1 \sigma_E^2 & \lambda_1 \lambda_2 \sigma_T^2 & \lambda_1 \lambda_3 \sigma_T^2 & \lambda_1 \lambda_4 \sigma_T^2 \\
\lambda_2 \lambda_1 \sigma_T^2 & \lambda_2^2 \sigma_T^2 + \lambda_2 \sigma_E^2 & \lambda_2 \lambda_3 \sigma_T^2 & \lambda_2 \lambda_4 \sigma_T^2 \\
\lambda_3 \lambda_1 \sigma_T^2 & \lambda_3 \lambda_2 \sigma_T^2 & \lambda_3^2 \sigma_T^2 + \lambda_3 \sigma_E^2 & \lambda_3 \lambda_4 \sigma_T^2 \\
\lambda_k \lambda_1 \sigma_T^2 & \lambda_4 \lambda_2 \sigma_T^2 & \lambda_4 \lambda_3 \sigma_T^2 & \lambda_4^2 \sigma_T^2 + \lambda_4 \sigma_E^2
\end{pmatrix}, \quad (3.5)
$$

where σ_E^2 is the composite (i.e., total) error variance. This matrix is the same as that in Equation 3.3 with the exception of effective test length parameters being included in the error variance term. This restriction does not affect the implications of congeneric measures, and the benefit of this added restriction is that simplified formulas may be used for estimating the reliability of classically congeneric scores.

Essentially τ-Equivalent Measures. If Equation 3.1 is restricted such that the true score from replication 1 is equal to the true score from replication 2 (i.e. have the same effective length parameter) plus a constant, then the replications are *essentially τ-equivalent.* Under this assumption, error variances are allowed to differ, but true score variance is the same for all parts. This implies that essentially τ-equivalent measures have (a) different expected observed scores; (b) equal true score variances; (c) different observed score variances; (d) the same covariance, but possibly different correlation between observed scores from any pair of essentially τ-equivalent measures; (e) the same covariance, but possibly different correlation, for any essentially τ-equivalent measure and an external measure; and (f) different reliabilities.

The observed score model for essentially τ-equivalent measures is given by, $X_{aj} = \lambda T_a + E_{aj} + c_j$. The difference between this equation and Equation 3.1 is that the effective length parameter (i.e. factor loading) is the same for all parts. As a result, each of the k parts contributes equally to the composite true score.

The part-test observed score covariance matrix is

$$
\begin{pmatrix}
(1/4)^2\sigma_T^2 + \sigma_{E_1}^2 & (1/4)^2\sigma_T^2 & (1/4)^2\sigma_T^2 & (1/4)^2\sigma_T^2 \\
(1/4)^2\sigma_T^2 & (1/4)^2\sigma_T^2 + \sigma_{E_2}^2 & (1/4)^2\sigma_T^2 & (1/4)^2\sigma_T^2 \\
(1/4)^2\sigma_T^2 & (1/4)^2\sigma_T^2 & (1/4)^2\sigma_T^2 + \sigma_{E_3}^2 & (1/4)^2\sigma_T^2 \\
(1/4)^2\sigma_T^2 & (1/4)^2\sigma_T^2 & (1/4)^2\sigma_T^2 & (1/4)^2\sigma_T^2 + \sigma_{E_4}^2
\end{pmatrix}.
$$

$$(3.6)$$

In Equation 3.6, each part contributes equally to the composite (i.e., total) true score variance. Therefore, each part's contribution to the composite true score variance may be expressed as $1/k$ times the composite true score variance. That is, the effective length parameter is $1/k$. Consequently, the off-diagonal elements (i.e., the covariance terms) are now equal, but the correlations among parts differ. For example, the correlation between part 1 and 2 is

$$
\frac{(1/4)^2\sigma_T^2}{\sigma_{X_1}\sigma_{X_2}},
$$

where $\sigma_{X_j} = \sqrt{(1/k)^2\sigma_T^2 + \sigma_{E_j}^2}$. The numerator of the correlation between any two parts will be the same, but the denominator will differ as a result of different part-test observed score variances. Like congeneric measures, the reliabilities will be different for each part, but this result is strictly due to the different error variances. The true score variances are the same for each part.

τ-Equivalent Measures. The assumption of *τ-equivalence* restricts the essentially *τ*-equivalent model by stipulating that true scores are the same for each replication, $T_{a1} = T_{a2}$, but error variances are allowed to differ. As a result, observed scores from each part must have the same expected value. These stipulations imply that (a) *τ*-equivalent measures have equal expected observed scores, (b) equal true score variances, and (c) different observed score variances. It also implies the items (d) through (f) that were listed for essentially *τ*-equivalent measures.

In terms of observed scores, τ-equivalent measures require that $X_{aj} = \lambda T_a + E_{aj}$ (note the missing constant). However, the covariance matrix turns out to be the same as the one for essentially τ-equivalent measures.

Parallel Measures. The oldest and most strict assumption is parallel measures. It requires parts to have (a) equal expected observed scores, (b) equal true score variances, (c) equal observed score variances, (d) the same covariance and correlation between observed scores from any pair of parallel measures, (e) the same covariance and correlation for any parallel measure and an external measure, and (f) equal reliabilities.

The observed score linear model for each parallel part is the same as that listed for τ-equivalent parts. However, the added assumption of equal error variances results in a different covariance matrix. The matrix for a four-part measure with parallel parts is:

$$\begin{pmatrix} (1/4)^2\sigma_T^2 + (1/4)\sigma_E^2 & (1/4)^2\sigma_T^2 & (1/4)^2\sigma_T^2 & (1/4)^2\sigma_T^2 \\ (1/4)^2\sigma_T^2 & (1/4)^2\sigma_T^2 + (1/4)\sigma_E^2 & (1/4)^2\sigma_T^2 & (1/4)^2\sigma_T^2 \\ (1/4)^2\sigma_T^2 & (1/4)^2\sigma_T^2 & (1/4)^2\sigma_T^2 + (1/4)\sigma_E^2 & (1/4)^2\sigma_T^2 \\ (1/4)^2\sigma_T^2 & (1/4)^2\sigma_T^2 & (1/4)^2\sigma_T^2 & (1/4)^2\sigma_T^2 + (1/4)\sigma_E^2 \end{pmatrix}.$$

$$(3.7)$$

In Equation 3.7, each part contributes equally to the composite (i.e., total) true score variance and composite error variance. Therefore, each part's contribution to the composite true score variance may be expressed as $1/k$ times the composite true score variance, and each part's contribution to the composite error score variance may be expressed as $1/k$ times the composite error score variance. That is, the effective length parameter is $1/k$. The difference between the matrix in Equation 3.7 and the one in Equation 3.6 is the equality of error variances. With equal error variances, not only are the covariance terms equal, but the corresponding correlations are equal and the part-test reliabilities are equal.

The assumption of parallel measures is the most restrictive, and it is arguably unlikely to hold in practice. If the assumption is tenable, however, all of the parts are interchangeable or, as noted by Gulliksen, "it makes no difference which one is used" (1950, p. 28). Lord and Novick wrote a similar description, "Parallel measurements measure exactly the same thing in the same scale and, in a sense, measure it equally well for all persons" (Lord & Novick, 1968, p. 48).

Violation of Essential τ-Equivalence

Internal consistency reliability coefficients such as Cronbach's α estimate the true reliability when measures are at least essentially τ-equivalent (i.e., essentially τ-equivalent, τ-equivalent, or parallel), the measure is unidimensional, and error scores are uncorrelated. These coefficients become lower bounds to true reliability under the assumption of congeneric measures (Lord & Novick, 1968). Violating the assumption of essential τ-equivalence and working with a lower bound to reliability is not difficult, provided that scores are unidimensional and error scores are uncorrelated. It typically leads to the following lower-bound line of reasoning: "my value of Cronbach's α is 0.8. This value is a lower bound, which indicates that the true reliability value is higher. Therefore, my scores are acceptably reliable." That is, as long as the lower bound is acceptably high, the true reliability is also acceptably high because it is guaranteed to be higher than the lower bound. This line of reasoning is only justified when scores are also unidimensional and have no correlated errors. Simultaneous violation of essential τ-equivalence and uncorrelated error may cause the reliability estimate to actually be an upper bound, not a lower bound! Under these circumstances, the lower-bound line of reasoning is fatally flawed and leads to erroneous conclusions. This consequence is another reason why evidence of unidimensionality and uncorrelated error should be obtained prior to estimating reliability. The tenability of the lower-bound line of reasoning rests on the veracity of these assumptions.

Statistical tests of parallel, τ-equivalence, and congeneric measures are possible through *confirmatory factor analysis* (CFA; see Jöreskog, 1971; Reuterberg & Gustafsson, 1992). The tenability of these assumptions may also be explored by careful consideration of scores produced from various splits of the data. For example, the most obvious violation of parallel measures occurs when each part contains a different number of items. Observed scores for each part cannot have equal means or variances when the number of items on each part is different. For example, Table 3.1 lists the descriptive statistics for the odd-even and content balanced partition of the ELA Benchmark Assessment into two parts. The means and variances for the two part-tests are more discrepant for the

Table 3.1

Descriptive Statistics for Two Part-Test Partitions and the Total Test

Partition	Test	Mean	Variance	Correlation[a]	Covariance
Odd-Even	Odd-Part	17.5	41.72	0.87	36.52
	Even-Part	16.73	42.53	–	–
Content	Part 1	15.93	37.68	0.87	36.41
	Part 2	18.06	46.79	–	–
None	Total	33.98	157.28	–	–

[a]Correlation and covariance computed between part-tests.

Content-based partition than for the Odd-Even partition, although the correlation and covariance between parts appear to be similar. These statistics also demonstrate the difficulty of balancing content while creating part-tests that are of equal length and reasonably parallel. The odd-even split results in part-test scores that are more likely to meet the assumption of parallel measures than the content-based split.

Another situation that may invalidate certain assumptions occurs when items are assigned a different number of points or weighted differently. For example, a test comprised of binary and polytomous items could result in part-tests that have very different maximum possible scores. A *maximum possible score* is the sum of the total number of points awarded by each item. As such, even when a test has an equal number of items, the maximum possible score may differ. In this situation, the assumption of parallel measures would be hard to justify. The two parts test would more likely be congeneric.

If one is uncertain whether scores are parallel, essentially τ-equivalent, or congeneric, then multiple estimates should be reported; one estimate that assumes essentially τ-equivalent scores and another that assumes congeneric measures. This practice will provide more evidence that supports the reliability of scores, provided that the measure is unidimensional and contains no error score correlations.

Classification Decisions and Generalizability Theory

Randomly Parallel Measures. Strong true score theory and generalizability theory assume that replications are randomly parallel. In strong true score theory, items are randomly parallel if the items that make up the measurement procedure are considered to be random samples from the domain (Lord, 1955a). Generalizability theory extends this notion to multifaceted sampling by assuming that observations from each facet are randomly sampled from the universe. For example, occasions and items are considered to be randomly sampled in a two-facet design.

Parallel and randomly parallel measures are distinct assumptions that lead to different results. Parallel measures underpin the early development of classical test theory model. It is a strict assumption that implies certain characteristics of the observed scores, such as equality of expected observed scores and equal observed score variances. Randomly parallel measures are parallel in content but "need not have equal means or equal variances" (Crocker & Algina, 1986, p. 124). Moreover, randomly parallel measures permit the use of alternative measurement models and possibly stronger distributional assumptions about scores.

Distributional Assumptions. Although strong true score theory and generalizability theory share the assumption of randomly parallel measures, they are very different with respect to distributional assumptions about scores. The assumption of randomly parallel measures justifies the use of the binomial distribution in strong true score theory (Equation 1.8), but it does not guarantee that the binomial distribution is appropriate. Statistical tests are available for evaluating model–data fit (see Lord, 1965), but careful consideration of item characteristics may also provide evidence in support of or contrary to the binomial distribution. First, the binomial distribution requires a constant probability of success for each item. Tests comprised of items that vary widely in difficulty are not likely to meet this requirement, and the score distribution may be better characterized by an item-response theory model (see Birnbaum, 1968). Second, only binary scored items are permitted. More complex distributions are suitable for polytomous items (i.e., items scored in an ordinal fashion such 1,

2, 3, or 4) and combinations of binary and polytomous items (see Lee, 2007). Distributional assumptions in strong true score theory necessitate careful consideration of model–data fit and other item characteristics, but no such considerations are necessary for generalizability theory. Generalizability theory is "weak" in the sense that it is distribution-free. Like classical test theory, it makes no distributional assumptions about scores. It is flexible and easily applied to binary or polytomous items.

Violation of Randomly Parallel Measures

Failing to randomly sample items from the domain does not necessarily result in a violation of the randomly parallel assumption. As long as items on a test are exchangeable with items in the domain, the assumption of randomly parallel measures is supported. An item is *exchangeable* if it makes no difference whether it is used on the test or some other item specified by the domain is used on the test. This notion is reflected in Cronbach, Gelser, Nanda, and Rajaratnam's defense of the randomly parallel assumption:

> The essential requirement for reasonable application of sampling theory is that the universe be defined clearly enough that one can recognize elements belonging to it .... A semantically and logically adequate definition will enable the consumer of research to consider possible candidates for membership in the universe, to judge whether the candidate is indeed included by the definition, and to reach the same conclusion as other interpreters of the definition. (Cronbach, Gleser, Nanda, & Rajaratnam, 1972, p. 368)

Kane (2002, p. 172) described this practice as representative sampling:

> If it can be plausibly claimed that the sample of conditions in the [generalizability] study is representative of a specified universe of admissible observations, then the [generalizability] study variance components can be linked to this universe. Further, if the universe of generalization employed in subsequent [decision] studies is equivalent to or is a subset

of this universe of admissible observations, the [generalizability] study variance components can be used to evaluate the dependability of inferences to this universe of generalization.

Therefore, justifying or refuting the assumption of randomly parallel measures often involves justifying exchangeability. If exchangeability can be established, the assumption of randomly parallel measures is supported; items may be considered a random sample from some model (Bernardo, 1996). If exchangeability cannot be established for a measurement procedure, then the wrong data collection design, and ultimately the wrong measurement model, is being used. Correcting a violation is thus a matter of identifying the data collection design for which exchangeability is tenable.

Item exchangeability is an appropriate assumption for a $p \times i$ design if items in the universe are of similar difficulty and content. Under these conditions, items are exchangeable and may be considered a random sample. However, if the content (denoted here as c) is deemed too variable, and the "true" design is a $p \times (i : c)$ design, item exchangeability is not tenable for the $p \times i$ design. Items that vary widely by content are only exchangeable under the $p \times (i : c)$ design or some other design that accounts for content area. The table of specifications model in multivariate generalizability theory is an example of an alternative design. Identifying a data collection design that satisfies exchangeability is aided by clearly defining the universe.

Exchangeability in a multifaceted measurement procedure, such as one that involves items and raters, requires careful specification of the universe. A replication of the measurement procedure should be exchangeable with any other replication. Therefore, test specifications should clearly define permissible items, and rater specifications should define permissible raters. For example, test specification might define item type and content area, and rater specifications might stipulate the type of rater, the rater training process, and ongoing rater quality-assurance procedures. Any replication conforming to these specifications may then be considered exchangeable with any other replication. A well-defined universe of admissible observations provides reassurance that the appropriate design has been identified and that replications of the measurement procedure are exchangeable.

Chapter Summary

All methods described in this text assume unidimensionality and uncorrelated error scores. Violating these assumptions may positively or negatively bias reliability estimates and lead to erroneous conclusions about the quality of test scores. Therefore, these assumptions should be tested prior to estimating reliability. Once the veracity of these assumptions has been evaluated, the nature of measurement procedure replications should be examined.

A variety of coefficients are available for scores that are assumed to be congeneric, classical congeneric, essentially τ-equivalent, τ-equivalent, randomly parallel, or parallel. Choosing the right coefficient depends in part on knowing which assumption is most tenable. Choosing the wrong coefficient can result in obtaining a lower bound to reliability (i.e., underestimating reliability).

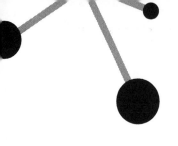

METHODS

4

INFORMATION UP TO this point in the text provides the context for knowing when each method of estimating reliability is appropriate. For this chapter, reliability coefficients are organized into decision trees in Figures 4.1 and 4.2 to facilitate an understanding of the conditions that led to their development and the selection of an appropriate coefficient. Details of these coefficients are explained in the body of this chapter. All of the coefficients listed in these figures require the assumptions of unidimensionality and uncorrelated errors. Figure 4.1 pertains to relative decisions (i.e., norm-referenced tests), and Figure 4.2 applies to absolute decisions (i.e., criterion-referenced tests). Each decision tree involves choices about the number of sources of error, the type of replication, the number of parts, and the underlying assumptions. Only those choices necessary for identifying a reliability coefficient are listed in the decision tree. For example, selecting a coefficient in generalizability theory only requires choices about the type of decision and the number of measurement error sources. The data collection design and the assumption of randomly parallel measures are not listed for generalizability theory because they do not provide additional help in choosing a generalizability theory coefficient over some other method. However, these latter two considerations are

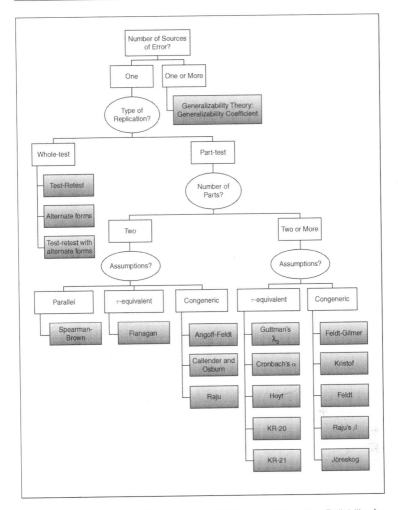

Figure 4.1. Decision Tree for Selecting a Method for Estimating Reliability for Relative Decisions

important for estimation and interpretation of a coefficient in generalizability theory. Some coefficients may be listed in more than one place, but for simplicity, coefficients are only listed in the place that requires the least restrictive assumption. For example, Cronbach's α is listed under τ-equivalent, but it could also have been listed under parallel.

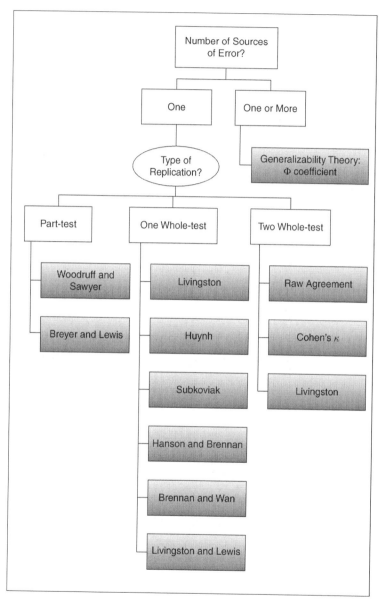

Figure 4.2. Decision Tree for Selecting a Method for Estimating Reliability for Absolute Decisions

Reliability Coefficients for Relative Decisions

Whole-Test Replications

Test-retest, alternate forms, and test-retest with alternate forms all involve the administration of a complete test form on two occasions. A coefficient of stability is obtained from the test-retest design described in Chapter 2 (see Table 2.2) by correlating scores from each occasion. Error scores will be large, and the reliability estimate will be low if the construct being measured changes a lot from one occasion to another. Conversely, error scores will be small and reliability will be high when the construct remains stable over time. Other sources of random variation also contribute to error but to a lesser extent. The design is primarily affected by random fluctuations of the construct. To assess error due to other sources, such as choice of test form, an alternate data collection design and coefficient is required.

A coefficient of equivalence involves two similar forms administered according to an alternate forms design (see Table 2.3). It is estimated by correlating scores from each form. The particular items chosen to create each form are the primary source of error reflected in this coefficient. Similar forms will have a high correlation, whereas dissimilar forms will have a low correlation.

A coefficient of stability and equivalence is obtained from the test-retest with alternate forms design (see Table 2.4). The estimate is affected by changes in the construct and (or) differences in test forms. However, the two sources of error are confounded. All of the error may be due to lack of stability, a lack of equivalence, or both. There is no way to differentiate the two sources of error. Therefore, the reliability estimate increases or decreases as stability and (or) equivalence increases or decreases.

As noted previously, designs that involve two whole-test replications are very expensive to implement. Reliability methods based on a single test administration are more common. These methods involve designs that divide a single test into two or more parts.

Two Part-Test Replications

Four different reliability methods are applicable to the data collection design involving two part-test replications (see Table 2.5).

The appropriateness of each method depends on the underlying assumptions. Given a measurement procedure split into two parallel parts, the *Spearman-Brown formula* (Brown, 1910; Spearman, 1910) should be used to adjust the part-test reliability estimate to reflect a whole-test reliability estimate. The Spearman-Brown formula is

$$\text{Spearman-Brown} = \frac{2\rho_{XX'}}{1 + \rho_{XX'}}, \tag{4.1}$$

where $\rho_{XX'}$ is the correlation between the two half-tests (i.e., the half-test score reliability). If the assumption of parallel measures is not tenable, the half-test reliability may be adjusted to full-test reliability using alternate methods.

Flanagan's formula (Rulon, 1939) is useful when the half-tests are assumed to be essentially τ-equivalent. It is computed from the observed score variance, σ_X^2, and the sum of the part variances, $\sum_{j=1}^{k} \sigma_{X_j}^2$,

$$\text{Flanagan} = 4\left(\frac{\sigma_X^2 - \sum_{j=1}^{2} \sigma_{X_j}^2}{\sigma_X^2}\right). \tag{4.2}$$

Flanagan's coefficient will be less than or equal to the Spearman-Brown estimate. However, the assumption of essential τ-equivalence is likely to be more tenable than the assumption of parallel measures—a condition that supports the use of Flanagan's estimate over the Spearman-Brown estimate.

Raju (1970) generalized Flanagan's estimate of reliability to account for the situation in which each of the two parts is comprised of a different number of items. The unequal length part-tests imply that the parts are congeneric and not essentially τ-equivalent or parallel. His coefficient requires that the length of the two parts be known. The *Raju formula* is given by

$$\text{Raju} = \frac{1}{\lambda_1 \lambda_2} \left(\frac{\sigma_X^2 - \sum_{j=1}^{2} \sigma_{X_j}^2}{\sigma_X^2} \right), \qquad (4.3)$$

where λ_1 is the proportion of items on the first part-test (i.e., $\lambda_1 = k_1/k$), and λ_2 is the proportion of items on the second part-test (i.e. $\lambda_2 = k_2/k$). The Flanagan and Raju estimates will depart to the extent that the numbers of items differ between the two part-tests. When the two part-tests contain the same number of items, Raju's formula is equivalent to Flanagan's formula.

Raju's formula uses known test length to relate true scores on the two part-tests. However, there are situations in which this relationship among true scores is better described by the unknown but effective test length. By assuming that the two parts are classical congeneric, the *Angoff-Feldt coefficient* (Angoff, 1953; Feldt, 1975) is computed by substituting the effective test lengths, $\lambda_1 = \left[\sigma_X^2 + (\sigma_{X_1}^2 - \sigma_{X_2}^2) \right]/2\sigma_X^2$, and $\lambda_2 = 1 - \lambda_1$, into Raju's formula (Equation 4.3).

A weakness of reliability methods based on a two part-test design is the influence of partition choice on the reliability estimate. There are many ways to divide a test into two parts, and each partition will result in a different reliability estimate. Reliability methods based on a multiple part-test design overcome this weakness.

Multiple Part-Test Replications

Cronbach solved the problem of deciding which two-part split was best for estimating reliability. He developed coefficient α (eponymously referred to as Cronbach's α) and showed that it was the average of all possible split-half Spearman-Brown reliability estimates (Cronbach, 1951). Cronbach's α is arguably the most well-known reliability coefficient for a multiple part-test data collection designs. It is suitable for binary and polytomous items or a combination of the two item types. Coefficient α is given by

$$\text{Cronbach's } \alpha = \left(\frac{k}{k-1} \right) \left(\frac{\sigma_X^2 - \sum_{j=1}^{k} \sigma_{X_j}^2}{\sigma_X^2} \right). \qquad (4.4)$$

If the assumption of essential τ-equivalence is tenable, Cronbach's α is an estimate of the reliability coefficient, but if scores are congeneric, it is a lower bound to reliability.

A special case of Cronbach's α is the *Kuder-Richardson formula 20* (KR-20; Kuder & Richardson, 1937). If all of the items are binary, Cronbach's α and the KR-20 are the same. Indeed, Equation 4.4 is properly referred to as the KR-20 when all of the test items are binary.

A further simplification is achieved when the average item covariance is used in lieu of the sum of item covariance. This simplification is known as the *Kuder-Richardson formula 21* (KR-21). It is an appropriate reliability method when items are similar in difficulty. The KR-21 is given by

$$\text{KR-21} = \left(\frac{k}{k-1} \right) \left[\frac{\mu_X (k - \mu_X)}{k\sigma_X} \right], \qquad (4.5)$$

where μ_X is the average observed score.

Guttman (1945) derived six lower bounds to reliability. His first lower bound was the ratio of the total covariance to total variance. His second lower bound is given by

$$\text{Guttman's } \lambda_2 = \left(\frac{\sqrt{\frac{k}{k-1} \left[\sigma_X^4 - \sum_{j=1}^{k} \sigma_{X_j}^4 \right]}}{\sigma_X^2} \right) + \left(\frac{\sigma_X^2 - \sum_{j=1}^{k} \sigma_{X_j}^2}{\sigma_X^2} \right),$$

$$(4.6)$$

and his third lower bound is equivalent to Cronbach's α. Guttman's λ_2 also equals Cronbach's α if all of the part-test covariances are equal. Otherwise, Guttman's λ_2 will be larger. As such, Guttman's λ_2 is a better lower bound to reliability than Cronbach's α, and for this reason it is preferred.

The assumption of τ-equivalent measures is not appropriate in many situations and, therefore, reliability is best estimated by methods that assume that measures are congeneric. Raju's β is an extension of his two-part coefficient to multiple parts. It too requires that the length of each congeneric part be known, and it may be computed for any item type or combination of item types. The coefficient is given by

$$
\text{Raju's } \beta = \left(\frac{1}{1 - \sum_{j=1}^{k} \lambda_j^2} \right) \left(\frac{\sigma_X^2 - \sum_{j=1}^{k} \sigma_{X_j}^2}{\sigma_X^2} \right), \quad (4.7)
$$

where λ_j is the proportion of items on part j. This coefficient is useful for tests composed of multiple item types, such as multiple-choice, constructed-response, and extended-response. Items can be grouped by type to form the part-tests. If it is reasonable to assume that each part-test contributes to the composite proportionally to the length of each part, Raju's β is appropriate. Otherwise, the Feldt-Gilmer or Feldt-Brennan classical congeneric method is a better choice.

Raju's β is a general form for reliability estimators. Many other reliability methods are special cases of Raju's β. They differ by definition of the effective test length parameters (i.e., the λ_j) as explained by Haertel (2006). For example, if the number of parts equals the number of test items (i.e., all $\lambda_j = 1/k$), Raju's β reduces to Cronbach's α.

Kristof (1974) extended Raju's β to part-tests of unknown length. His coefficient provides a method for estimating reliability for classical congeneric measures for any item type or combination of item types. However, it is limited to a three-part division of the test. Gilmer and Feldt (Gilmer & Feldt, 1983) proposed a coefficient for classical congeneric measures that does not limit the number of part-tests. The *Feldt-Gilmer coefficient* is given by

$$
\text{Feldt-Gilmer} = \left(\frac{\left(\sum_{j=1}^{k} D_j \right)^2}{\left(\sum_{j=1}^{k} D_j \right)^2 - \sum_{j=1}^{k} D_j^2} \right) \left(\frac{\sigma_X^2 - \sum_{j=1}^{k} \sigma_{X_j}^2}{\sigma_X^2} \right),
$$

$$(4.8)$$

where
$$
D_j = \frac{\sum\limits_{g=1}^{h} \sigma_{X_j X_g} - \sigma_{X_j X_\ell} - \sigma_{X_j}^2}{\sum\limits_{g=1}^{h} \sigma_{X_\ell X_g} - \sigma_{X_j X_\ell} - \sigma_{X_\ell}^2}.
$$

Row ℓ is the row of the covariance matrix with the largest sum of covariances. If $j = \ell$, then $D_j = 1$. When the number of part-tests is three, the Feldt-Gilmer and Kristof coefficients are the same. The Feldt-Gilmer coefficient requires numerous computations. An easier-to-compute alternative is the Feldt-Brennan classical congeneric coefficient.

Feldt and Brennan (1989) described a formula for estimating reliability under the assumption of classical congeneric measures. It is appropriate for any item type or combination of item types. *Feldt's classical congeneric reliability coefficient* is given by

$$
\text{Feldt-Brennan} = \left(\frac{1}{1 - \sum_{j=1}^{k} \sigma_{X_j X} / \sigma_X^2} \right) \left(\frac{\sigma_X^2 - \sum_{j=1}^{k} \sigma_{X_j}^2}{\sigma_X^2} \right), \quad (4.9)
$$

where $\sigma_{X_j X}$ is the covariance between part j and the total test score. This method is somewhat easier to compute than the Feldt-Gilmer coefficient, but in some cases it overestimates reliability (Osburn, 2000).

Other Methods for Estimating Reliability

Generalizability theory provides the only coefficient suitable for situations that involve multiple sources of error. The generalizability coefficient (Equation 1.28) is the general form, but a wide variety of error sources may be characterized by the error term in this coefficient. Therefore, it should always be interpreted with respect to the universe of generalization.

Two coefficients listed in Figure 4.1 but not described in detail are those developed by Callendar and Osburn (1979) and Jöreskog (1971). Both methods are iterative and cannot be computed by a simple formula. The method by Callendar and Oshburn tends to be robust to violation of unidimensionality (Osburn, 2000), but the confirmatory factor analysis method of Jöreskog is more general and allows reliability to be computed for parallel, τ-equivalent, and congeneric measures that are unidimensional or multidimensional. Moreover, Jöreskog's method provides a statistical test of the assumptions underlying test scores.

Not listed in Figure 4.1 is *stratified* α. This coefficient is useful when items may be grouped according to content area or subtest. Stratified α is recommended if scores are believed to be multidimensional with simple structure or when composite scores are computed for a test battery. Given a composite $s = 1, \ldots, t$ of subtests (i.e., strata), this estimate is computed by first estimating reliability and observed score variance for each subtest. These values are then pooled together in a composite reliability estimate given by

$$\text{Stratified } \alpha = 1 - \frac{\sum_{s=1}^{t} \sigma_{X_s}^2 (1 - \alpha_s)}{\sigma_X^2} \qquad (4.10)$$

where $\sigma_{X_s}^2$ is the observed score variance and α_s is Cronbach's α for subtest s. The observed score variance for the entire composite is σ_X^2.

Estimating Reliability for Absolute Decisions

A decision tree for selecting a reliability coefficient for absolute decisions is presented in Figure 4.2. It involves decisions about

(a) the number of sources of error and (b) the type of replication. Most of the coefficients listed in the figure require the assumption of randomly parallel measures. The exception is Livingston's coefficient, which requires an assumption of parallel measures.

An absolute decision involves the classification of examinees according to an absolute standard, such as an achievement-level cut score. It is possible and perfectly acceptable for all examinees to have the same achievement level. Tests designed for absolute decisions can consistently classify examinees even when there is no true score variance. Reliability coefficients for relative decision would all be low due to a lack of heterogeneity among true scores. Therefore, absolute decisions require coefficients that can be high even when there is little to no true score variance.

Squared error loss and threshold loss methods are more appropriate indicators of reliability for absolute decisions. Decision consistency methods, in particular, describe how consistently examinees are classified upon replication of the measurement procedure. The methods described below presume that the $l = 0, \ldots, L$ cut scores, denoted by $C_0, C_l, \ldots, C_L$, are boundaries for the $b = 0, \ldots, B$ achievement levels. Note that the lowest cut score equals zero, $C_0 = 0$, and the highest cut score equals the total number of items plus one, $C_L = n + 1$.

Two Whole-Test Replications

Squared Error Loss Coefficients. Livingston (1972) proposed a squared error loss method that is applicable to one or two whole-test replications that are parallel. The idea behind his coefficient is that reliability of a criterion-referenced test increases as the group mean deviates from a cut score. This deviation is expressed as $\mu_X - C_X$ for form X. If the group mean is at the cut score, *Livingston's coefficient* reduces to an alternate forms estimate of reliability. His coefficient remains positive even if true score variance is small or zero, which may happen in settings in which examinees are trained to a particular standard. Given scores obtained from two parallel forms, X and Y, Livingston's coefficient is given by

$$\text{Livingston} = \frac{\sigma_{XY} + (\mu_X - C_X)(\mu_Y - C_Y)}{\sqrt{[\sigma_X^2 + (\mu_X - C_X)^2][\sigma_Y^2 + (\mu_Y - C_Y)^2]}}. \quad (4.11)$$

As shown in the next section, a simpler version of this formula is applicable to a data collection design that involves one whole-test replication.

Threshold Loss Indices. Decision consistency indices are an alternative to squared error loss methods. These methods evaluate how well examinees are classified into achievement levels defined by one or more cut scores. A two-way table forms the basis of decision consistency indices. Rows of this table represent the proportion of examinees in each achievement level for one replication, and the columns represent the same information for the second replication. Each cell in the table represents the joint achievement levels for both replications. Entries in each cell are the proportion of examinees classified into achievement levels on both replications. Table 4.1 is an example of two replications that have four achievement levels: Below Basic, Basic, Proficient, and Advanced.

Hambleton and Novick (1973) recommended raw agreement as a measure of decision consistency. Raw agreement indicates the proportion of examinees who were classified in the same

Table 4.1

Example Notation for a Two-way Table of Achievement-level Classification

		Replication 2				
		Below Basic	Basic	Proficient	Advanced	
Replication 1	Below Basic	p_{00}	p_{01}	p_{02}	p_{03}	$p_{1\cdot}$
	Basic	p_{10}	p_{11}	p_{12}	p_{13}	$p_{2\cdot}$
	Proficient	p_{20}	p_{21}	p_{22}	p_{23}	$p_{3\cdot}$
	Advanced	p_{30}	p_{31}	p_{32}	p_{33}	$p_{4\cdot}$
		$p_{\cdot 1}$	$p_{\cdot 2}$	$p_{\cdot 3}$	$p_{\cdot 4}$	$p_{\cdot\cdot}$

way on both replications. It is obtained by summing the proportions on the diagonal from upper left to lower right. Specifically,

$$P_{Raw} = \sum_{b=0}^{B} p_{bb}. \qquad (4.12)$$

In terms of table 4.1, $P_{Raw} = P_{00} + P_{11} + P_{22} + P_{33}$. Raw agreement has a simple interpretation. It is the proportion of examinees consistently classified. For example, a raw agreement of .8 indicates that 80% of examinees were classified consistently. This coefficient is easy to compute, but it requires that the same test be administered on two occasions (i.e., replication 1 and replication 2).

A limitation of the raw agreement index is that a certain amount of agreement is expected by chance. To overcome this limitation, Swaminathan, Hambleton, and Algina (1975) recommended *Cohen's κ* (Cohen, 1960) to describes the improvement in agreement beyond chance. This coefficient is computed by comparing the observed agreement to the agreement expected by chance. Observed agreement is computed by Equation 4.12. Chance agreement is computed by summing the product of margins,

$$P_{Chance} = \sum_{b=0}^{B} p_{b.}p_{.b}. \qquad (4.13)$$

In terms of table 4.1, $P_{Chance} = P_{0.}P_{.0} + P_{1.}P_{.1} + P_{2.}P_{.2} + P_{3.}P_{.3}$. Cohen's κ is then computed by,

$$\kappa = \frac{P_{Raw} - P_{Chance}}{1 - P_{Chance}}. \qquad (4.14)$$

It is interpreted as the improvement in agreement over chance. For example, $\kappa = .3$ indicates that the observed agreement is a 30% improvement over chance. Like the raw agreement index, Cohen's κ requires two administrations of the same test. This practice is usually cost prohibitive. Therefore, methods that rely on a single test administration are more common.

One Whole-Test Replication

Squared Error Loss Coefficients. Livingston's squared error loss method may also be computed for one whole-test replication. It is computed by

$$\text{Livingston} = \frac{\rho_{XT}^2 \sigma_X^2 + (\mu_X - C_X)^2}{\sigma_X^2 + (\mu_X - C_X)^2}, \qquad (4.15)$$

where an estimate of reliability is substituted for ρ_{XT}^2. This method of computing Livingston's coefficient is more likely to be encountered in practice than Equation 4.11, given that only one replication need be observed.

Brennan and Kane (1977) extended Livingston's coefficient to data collection designs that involve multiple sources of error. Their coefficient is based on an absolute error term, $\sigma^2(\Delta)$, computed via generalizability theory. Specifically, their coefficient is given by

$$\Phi(C) = \frac{\sigma^2(p) + (\mu - C)^2}{\sigma^2(p) + (\mu - C)^2 + \sigma^2(\Delta)}. \qquad (4.16)$$

An unbiased estimator of Equation 4.16 is obtained by substituting $(\overline{X} - C)^2 - \hat{\sigma}^2(\overline{X})$ for $(\mu - C)^2$ (Feldt & Brennan, 1989). The quantity $\hat{\sigma}^2(\overline{X})$ is an estimate of the variability of using $\overline{X}$ as an estimator of μ. Equation 4.16 achieves its lower limit and reduces to the Φ-coefficient (Equation 1.29) when the cut score is equal to the mean. The Φ-coefficient is a suitable alternative when a lower bound is acceptable.

Threshold Loss Indices. Decision consistency indices from one whole-test replication rely heavily on strong true score theory. An observed replication is compared to a hypothetical replication that is derived through distributional assumptions. Subkoviak (1976) proposed a method based on the binomial error model, and Huynh (1976a, 1976b) developed procedures based on the beta-binomial model. Subkoviak's method is somewhat easier to compute, but Huynh's methods have a number of more desirable properties, such as analytically derived standard errors (Subkoviak, 1978).

Subkoviak's raw agreement index describes the probability that an examinee, indexed by a, is assigned to the same achievement level on two randomly parallel measures (Subkoviak, 1976). His coefficient is appropriate for binary scored items and observed scores that fit a binomial error model. Each measure consists of n items. Only one test administration is necessary. The second randomly parallel measure is hypothetical. It may be computed for one or more cut scores using the binomial error model (Equation 1.8). Specifically, examinee a's raw agreement is

$$P_a = \sum_{l=1}^{L} P_l(C_{l-1} \leq X < C_l)^2. \qquad (4.17)$$

The sum on the right-hand side of Equation 4.17 is the total probability of observing a score between two cut scores (lower inclusive) for an examinee with domain score θ_a, $P_l(C_{l-1} \leq X < C_l) = \Sigma_{x=C_{l-1}}^{C_l} \binom{n}{x} \theta_a^x (1 - \theta_a)^{n-x}$. Note that $C_0 = 0$ and $C_L = n + 1$. Subkoviak recommended the Kelley regression estimate (Equation 1.12) be substituted for the domain score, but the maximum likelihood estimate is also feasible (see Chapter 1). An overall raw agreement index is obtained by averaging over all N examinees,

$$P_{Subkoviak} = \frac{1}{N} \sum_{a=1}^{N} P_a. \qquad (4.18)$$

A standard error for Subkoviak's agreement index may be obtained by the *bootstrap procedure* (see Efron & Tibshirani, 1993).

Huynh (1976a, 1976b) also developed methods involving one observed whole-test replication and a second hypothetical replication. For his method, items comprising each replication are assumed to be exchangeable observations from the domain of items (hence, randomly parallel). True scores are assumed to follow a two-parameter beta distribution, and the marginal distribution of observed scores for either replication is a beta-binomial (Equation 1.9). Huynh showed that the joint distribution of both replications is the bivariate beta-binomial,

$$f(x,y) = \frac{\binom{n}{x}\binom{n}{y}}{B(\alpha,\beta)} B(\alpha + x + y, 2n + \beta - x - y), \quad (4.19)$$

where the parameters α and β are given by Equations 1.10 and 1.11, respectively. These parameters can be estimated using scores from the observed replication. Huynh's raw agreement index is computed by summing Equation 4.19 over all pairs of x and y values between two cut scores (lower inclusive) and then summing these values over all achievement levels,

$$P_{Huynh} = \sum_{l=1}^{L} \sum_{x,y=C_{l-1}}^{C_l - 1} f(x,y). \quad (4.20)$$

Chance agreement is computed from the marginal density,

$$P_{Huynh-Chance} = \sum_{l=1}^{L} \left[\sum_{x=C_{l-1}}^{C_l - 1} h(x) \right]^2, \quad (4.21)$$

where $h(x)$ is given by Equation 1.9. Like Subkoviak's method, $C_0 = 0$ and $C_L = n + 1$. Huynh's κ is computed from Equations 4.20 and 4.21,

$$\text{Huynh's } \kappa = \frac{P_{Huynh} - P_{Huynh-Chance}}{1 - P_{Huynh-Chance}}. \quad (4.22)$$

This coefficient is interpreted in the same way as Cohen's κ, but it can be computed from a single test administration.

Other Methods

Figure 4.2 lists several methods that were not described in detail. These methods are viable and sometimes better alternatives than the Livingston, Subkoviak, or Huynh methods. For example, Hanson and Brennan (1990) proposed a method based on the four-parameter beta-binomial distribution. The four-parameter beta-binomial distribution tends to fit scores better than the two-parameter beta-binomial distribution. As such, the Hanson and Brennan method tends to perform better than either Subkoviak's or Huynh's method.

All of the strong true score theory indices make strong distributional assumptions about the scores. If these distributional assumptions are not tenable, methods that use them are not appropriate. Brennan and Wan (2004) developed a method similar to Subkoviak's procedure that makes no distributional assumptions. The items scores, or groups of item scores, must be independently and identically distributed, but the distributional form need not be specified. The unknown distribution of scores is estimated by the bootstrap procedure (Efron & Tibshirani, 1993), and an agreement index is computed from this distribution.

Chapter Summary

A variety of methods exist for estimating score reliability. Selecting an appropriate coefficient depends on the (a) type of decision, (b) the number of sources of error, (c) the type of replication, (d) the number of parts, and (e) the underlying assumptions. Decision trees presented in this chapter facilitate the selection of an appropriate coefficient, as well as an understanding of the conditions that led to their development. However, it is not necessary to select only one coefficient. Multiple coefficients should be reported, if necessary, to describe all salient sources of error or if there is uncertainty about the underlying assumptions.

5

RESULTS

AN UNDESIRABLE TREND in the social science literature is the large amount of work that lacks adequate documentation of reliability (Qualls & Moss, 1996; Thompson & Vacha-Haase, 2000; Vacha-Haase, Kogan, & Thompson, 2000; Whittington, 1998). Perhaps a lack of understanding about reliability is one reason for this deficiency. Another reason may be that many articles and texts on reliability focus on theory and estimation but lack an explanation of how to document the results. The exception is the *Standards for Educational and Psychological Testing* (*Standards*; American Educational Research Association et al., 1999), which provide thorough guidance on documenting reliability and other technical characteristics of a measurement procedure. To facilitate the proper documentation of reliability, a four-point outline extrapolated from the *Standards* is provided below.

After discussing the outline, three example reliability reports that cover a variety of real-world measurement procedures are presented. The first example involves the Benchmark assessment of English Language Arts (ELA). It builds on the ELA examples discussed in previous chapters. The second example is based on the South Carolina Palmetto Achievement Challenge Test (PACT) of mathematics (see Huynh, Meyer, & Barton, 2000). This test was part of the state's high-stakes testing program from 1999 to 2008. PACT scores are reported in a norm-referenced and criterion-referenced manner. It is included as an example of documenting coefficients that support relative and absolute decisions. The final example is based on an observational measure referred to as the MSCAN. No multiple-choice or objectively scored items are part of this measure. Rather, observers view a classroom lesson and assign a score. This measure is in development, and the analysis is conducted to evaluate the reliability of scores and investigate potential improvements in the amount of time needed to obtain ratings. Taken together, the Benchmark, PACT, and MSCAN examples cover a variety of measurement procedures and illustrate the documentation of reliability.

Documentation of Score Reliability

Complete reliability documentation requires more than reporting an estimate of reliability. It requires a description of the measurement procedure, with specific mention of all major sources of error and factors that affect reliability. This information provides context for judging the quality of an analysis, interpreting the results, and comparing reliability estimates from different measurement procedures. Documentation of score reliability should (a) characterize the examinee population and all major subpopulations, (b) describe the measurement procedure and all major sources of error, (c) present evidence in support of assumptions or discuss the consequences of unsupported assumptions, and (d) provide estimates of reliability and the standard error of measurement. These four points provide a general structure for reporting the results of a reliability analysis. Excluded from these four points are two practices that should not be a part of any reliability documentation: reporting evaluative statements about an estimate and justifying the consistency of scores through reliability induction.

Reliability documentation should be free of evaluation or judgment, thus allowing the reader to form an unbiased opinion of the quality of the measurement procedure. Statements such as, "Cronbach's α was .8, indicating a high level of reliability," should be avoided. The reader should be free to judge whether or not a value of .8 is indeed high. One exception to this rule is when the analysis is being conducted to improve the measurement procedure. A decision study designed to improve the efficiency of a measurement procedure by reducing the number of items is an example. In this case, results may be used to support recommended improvements or revisions to the measurement procedure.

Information about score reliability should be provided for every administration of a measurement procedure. This recommendation pertains to new measures and those with a long history of use. Reporting a reliability coefficient computed from a previous administration or the test manual as evidence of test reliability for the current administration is inadequate and does not justify the consistency of scores. Only in very specific circumstances is such a reliability induction justified (Vacha-Haase et al., 2000). As such, the best practice is to avoid it altogether and report reliability for every administration of a measurement procedure. The tested population may vary too much from one administration to another to justify reliability induction.

Characterize the Examinee Population

Reliability coefficients are affected by the examinee population. This result is evident in the expression for the reliability coefficient (Equation 1.3); true score variance is in the numerator and true score variance plus error is in the denominator. For a fixed amount of error variance, reliability will be large for a population with large true score variance (i.e., a heterogeneous population), but small for a population with small true score variance (i.e., a homogeneous population). Interpretation of reliability cannot be divorced from the examinee population. Therefore, documentation should characterize the examinee population through demographics and test score descriptive statistics, such as the mean and standard deviation.

Reporting overall demographics and descriptive statistics for a sample of examinees is appropriate when examinees represent a well-defined population. However, examinees often represent important subpopulations, such as gender and race. If these subpopulations differ with respect to reliability, an overall estimate of reliability may be positively or negatively biased (Waller, 2008). Therefore, demographics and descriptive statistics should be reported for each subpopulation, along with group-specific estimates of reliability and the standard error of measurement. This practice is specifically addressed in Standard 2.11, which states that a reliability estimate, standard error of measurement, and conditional standard error of measurement should be reported for any subpopulations for which these statistics may differ.

Describe the Measurement Procedure and All Major Sources of Error

Documentation should describe the measurement procedure in enough detail to justify the chosen methods and identify limitations of the reliability analysis. As noted in Chapter 1, measurement involves more than the test itself. It involves the entire testing situation and the process that produces test scores. Some features of the measurement procedure are fixed through standardization, but many others are not and may contribute to random measurement error. All major sources of error should be documented whether or not the magnitude of the error was evaluated in the analysis. In this manner, the selected methods can be justified and limitations of the analysis can be identified. Features of the measurement procedure that require special attention are the data collection design and method of item scoring.

Chapter 2 discussed data collection designs at length. This information is relevant for documenting reliability because it is through the data collection design that major sources of error are isolated. A description of the data collection design is a description of the source (or sources) of error reflected in the reliability estimate. It bears on the interpretation of an estimate and the comparability of different estimates. A test-retest design is not interpreted in the same manner as an alternate forms design. More importantly, a test-retest reliability estimate is not comparable to an alternate forms reliability estimate. The two coefficients reflect different sources of error. In a similar fashion, standard errors of measurement from the two designs are not comparable. Each reflects a different source of error. Standard 2.5 specifically addresses the issue of measurement error sources and the comparability of reliability coefficients and the comparability of standard errors of measurement. A final benefit of describing the data collection design is that sources of error included in a description of the measurement procedure but not listed as part of the data collection design suggest a limitation of the analysis.

A description of a measurement procedure that involves subjective scoring, such as raters judging the quality of a musical audition or observers assessing the quality of classroom lesson, requires special attention. Rater training and monitoring are an important part of the measurement procedure (Johnson, Penny, & Gordon, 2009). These processes should be described to reveal sources of error that may or may not be included in a data collection design. In many large-scale assessment situations, rater data are not collected in a way that conforms to a fully crossed or partially nested design, thus making a rigorous generalizability theory analysis difficult. Nevertheless, rater training and monitoring should be reported to identify limitations of the analysis. Standard 2.10 specifically addresses documentation of scores that involve subjective judgment. Item scoring for objectively scored items must also be documented.

A description of the item type (i.e., item scoring) is relevant to the chosen method of estimating reliability and the tenability of assumptions underlying the nature of measurement procedure replications. Some methods of estimating reliability, such as the KR-20, are restricted binary items. Other methods, such as Cronbach's α, are suitable for binary and polytomous items. A description of the item type is necessary to justify the selected coefficient. It also helps identify any violation of the underlying assumptions.

A test comprised of binary items is not likely to meet the assumption of parallel measures unless the items are very similar in difficulty. Likewise, a test composed of binary and polytomous items is more likely to meet the assumption of congeneric measures than any other assumption. This result is due to the different scale of each item. A split of the test that has binary items on one part and polytomous items on another may result in parts that have different average observed scores and different observed score variances. True scores cannot be expected to be the same in such a case as well. Describing the item types is a way to provide evidence in support of the underlying assumptions and justify a selected method of estimating reliability.

Present Evidence in Support of Assumptions

Chapter 3 contains a description of various assumptions and the consequences for violating them. Empirical evidence, or lack thereof, should be provided in reliability documentation. This information is necessary for understanding the value of a reliability coefficient. For example, if the assumptions of unidimensionality, uncorrelated errors, and congeneric measures are supported, then Cronbach's α may be interpreted as a lower bound. However, if the assumption of uncorrelated error is violated, Cronbach's α is most likely an upper bound. A seemingly small difference in the underlying assumptions results in a completely contrary interpretation of a reliability estimate. Therefore, evidence of the tenability of underlying assumption should be documented. Evidence in the form of a formal statistical test is preferred, but in many cases such a test is not possible.

The assumptions of unidimensionality and uncorrelated errors are the most difficult to handle. Large sample sizes and sophisticated statistical methods are needed to perform a rigorous statistical test of these assumptions. A small sample or lack of statistical training may preclude a rigorous statistical test of unidimensionality and uncorrelated errors. However, some evidence may be brought to bear on these assumptions by describing the construct, content, and measurement procedure. Perusal of part-test covariance matrices may also provide additional empirical evidence. When evidence for the assumptions is not based on a formal statistical test, the limitations of the evidence should be described along with the consequences of violating them. In this way, a reader is properly cautioned.

The assumption of parallel, τ-equivalent, and congeneric measures should also be formally tested if possible. However, an easier solution is to report reliability coefficients for each type of assumption. For example, Guttman's λ_2 and the Feldt-Gilmer coefficient can be reported to cover the assumptions of τ-equivalent and congeneric measures. This practice addresses any bias due to the nature of measurement procedure replications, as long as the assumptions of unidimensionality and uncorrelated errors are substantiated.

Provide Estimates of Reliability and the Standard Error of Measurement

Once the measurement procedure has been described and the factors that affect reliability have been addressed, estimates of reliability and the standard error of measurement should be documented. Reporting a single estimate of reliability and the standard error of measurement is rarely, if ever, adequate. If using a classical test theory approach, multiple coefficients should be reported to address multiple sources of error. Alternatively, a coefficient from a single generalizability theory design that accommodates all major sources of error can be reported. Multiple sources of error, however, are not the only reason to report multiple coefficients. According to Standard 2.1, reliability and the standard error of measurement should be reported for each type of score (e.g., raw score, scale score, subscale score) reported for a measurement procedure. If an analysis involves multiple methods of estimating reliability, then each method of estimating reliability, standard error of measurement, and conditional standard error of measurement should be described clearly, and each should be interpreted with respect to the type of error described by each statistic (see Standard 2.4). For tests that involve cut scores, decision consistency or squared error loss estimates of reliability should be reported (see Standard 2.15).

In addition to reporting a traditional standard error of measurement for each source of error and each reported scale, a conditional standard error of measurement should be reported. Standard 2.14 recommends that conditional standard errors of measurement should be reported across the range of true scores, with particular mention of the standard error at any cut score that is part of a measurement procedure.

An important caveat to any reported estimate of reliability is the influence of sampling error. Reliability and the standard error of measurement describe the influence of sampling items or some other source of measurement error. Estimates, however, are also influenced by the sampling of examinees. A group of examinees represents just one possible sample from a given population. Like other statistics, reliability is subject to (examinee) random sampling variability. For example, the Benchmark ELA assessment targets the population of eight graders in South Carolina. Eighth graders participating in the assessment during 2006 and eighth graders participating during 2007 represent two different samples from the population. Reliability estimates will vary for these two groups simply because of sampling variability. More confidence in the value of a reliability coefficient may be obtained through an interval estimate that accounts for sampling variability. Confidence intervals for the KR-20 and Cronbach's α may be computed with the analytically derived sampling distributions (see Feldt, 1965; Feldt, Woodruff, & Salih, 1987), and confidence intervals for other coefficients may be computed by the bootstrap method (see Efron & Tibshirani, 1993). Reliability confidence intervals should be reported whenever possible (Fan & Thompson, 2001).

Benchmark ELA Assessment

Sample Results Section

Eighth grade students participating in the Benchmark Assessment of ELA were 49% male and 45% female (see Table 5.1). The white (28%) and black (59%) groups comprised the majority of the sample by race. Other race groups represented about 8% of the sample. Demographics were missing for about 5% of the sample. Students scored about 30 points on average, of a maximum possible score of 64 points, but the average score ranged by about 9 points across groups. The standard deviation was comparable across all groups.

A confirmatory factor analysis of tetrachoric correlations supported the assumption of unidimensionality (details not shown). The assumption of uncorrelated errors was not specifically tested.

Table 5.1

English Language Arts (ELA) Benchmark Group Descriptive Statistics

Group	N	Mean	S.D.	KR-21
All	6,649	29.96	11.65	.8966
Male	3,280	31.48	11.29	.8884
Female	3,016	28.67	11.85	.9014
White	1,884	35.94	11.92	.9032
Black	3,915	27.26	10.31	.8663

Note: Demographics were missing for about 5% of the examinees.

However, a preliminary analysis included testlets, the most likely sources of correlated errors, to evaluate the influence of this facet on the results.

A person by items within testlet within occasion design, $p \times (i : t : o)$, resulted in little variance due to testlet. Moreover, a person by items within testlet $p \times (i : t)$ design produced results similar to those listed in Table 5.2 for the person by items nested within occasion $p \times (i : o)$ design. Taken together, these results suggest that the testlet and occasion effect are not unique and that a design that includes testlet or occasion (but not both) would suffice. Therefore, the analysis focused on the $p \times (i : o)$ design.

Variance components from the generalizability study are listed in Table 5.2. Person variance accounted for 11% of the total variance. In contrast, occasion represented a negligible amount of a variance, and items within occasion accounted for only 5% of the variance. The largest source of error variance was the residual. Across groups, person variance ranged from 8% to 12% of the total variance (see Table 5.3). Variance due to the residual was consistently the largest amount of error variance, and variance due to items nested within occasions was the second largest source of error variance across all groups.

A goal of the analysis was to improve the efficiency of the measurement procedure without sacrificing score reliability.

Table 5.2

Generalizability Study Variance Components for the ELA Benchmark

Component	Variance	Percent of Total
Persons, p	0.0272	11
Occasions, O	0.0000	0
Items : Occasions, $I : O$	0.0137	5
Persons $\times$ Occasions, pO	0.0072	3
Persons $\times$ Items : Occasions, $p(I : O)$	0.2017	81
Total	0.2498	100

Table 5.3

Generalizability Study Results for the ELA Benchmark by Group
(Percents in Parentheses)

Component	Male	Female	White	Black
p	0.0253 (10)	0.0283 (11)	0.0289 (12)	0.0198 (8)
O	0.000 (0)	0.0000 (0)	0.0000 (0)	0.0000 (0)
$I : O$	0.0169 (7)	0.0114 (5)	0.0178 (7)	0.0130 (5)
pO	0.0069 (3)	0.0073 (3)	0.0076 (3)	0.0069 (3)
$p(I : O)$	0.2013 (80)	0.2015 (81)	0.1910 (78)	0.2063 (84)
Total	0.2504 (100)	0.2485 (100)	0.2453 (100)	0.2460 (100)

Generalizability coefficients and standard errors of measurement
(i.e., relative error) were estimated for 12 different data collection
designs. Each design improves efficiency by reducing occasions,
items within occasions, or both (see Table 5.4). Results for each
alternative design should be compared to results for the observed
data collection design (Design 1).

Reducing the total number of items from 64 to 56 by eliminating one item per testlet reduced reliability from .8015 to .7910.
If content coverage is not adversely affected, efficiency could be
gained by using Design 2 instead of Design 1.

Fixing the occasion increases reliability. Indeed, fixing occasion
and reducing the total number of items to 48 by eliminating two
items per testlet results in a reliability estimate that is larger than
the estimate for the observed design. However, such a drastic
reduction of items would likely affect test content and result in a
test that does not accurately represent the table of specifications.
Fixing the occasion facet would also require that every school
administer the test on the same two occasions. Unfortunately,
such a standardization would likely result in fewer schools volun-
teering for the Benchmark program.

Consolidating the assessment to one occasion does not appear
to be a sensible approach. Generalizability coefficients are no
better than .7251 for all designs that involve a single random
occasion. If all participating schools administered the assessment
on the same day, test occasion would be fixed, and reliability

Table 5.4
Decision Study Results for the ELA Benchmark Using Relative Error

Design	Items (n'_i)	Occasions (n'_o)	Occasions	Generalizability Coefficient	SEM[a]
1	32	2	Random	.8015	0.0833
2	28	2	Random	.7910	0.0847
3	24	2	Random	.7775	0.0882
4	32	2	Fixed	.9070	0.0561
5	28	2	Fixed	.8952	0.0600
6	24	2	Fixed	.8798	0.0648
7	64	1	Random	.7251	0.1015
8	56	1	Random	.7164	0.1037
9	48	1	Random	.7053	0.1066
10	64	1	Fixed	.9159	0.0561
11	56	1	Fixed	.9050	0.0600
12	48	1	Fixed	.8909	0.0648

[a]Standard error of measurement of average scores
Note: These results are very similar to results from an analysis that included a testlet facet. Results from the more parsimonious model are provided for simplicity and brevity.

would be .89 or higher. However, the same problems with fixing occasions would persist for these single-occasion designs.

Decision study results for each group exhibited a similar pattern to the results for the entire sample (Table 5.5). Estimates tended to be higher for females than males and higher for white examinees than black examinees. Results for the male, female, and white group were comparable and consistently higher than results for the black group.

Given the influence of occasion, the conditional standard error of measurement was computed separately for each day of testing (Fig. 5.1). Testing on day 2 had a slightly lower conditional standard error of measurement than testing on day 1.

Table 5.5

Decision Study Generalizability Coefficients ($\epsilon\rho^2$) for the ELA Benchmark by Group using Relative Error

Design	Male $\epsilon\rho^2$	Male SEM	Female $\epsilon\rho^2$	Female SEM	White $\epsilon\rho^2$	White SEM	Black $\epsilon\rho^2$	Black SEM
1	.7933	0.0066	.8061	0.0068	.8104	0.0068	.7484	0.0067
2	.7823	0.0070	.7959	0.0073	.8008	0.0072	.7356	0.0071
3	.7681	0.0076	.7827	0.0079	.7884	0.0078	.7192	0.0078
4	.9013	0.0031	.9102	0.0032	.9164	0.0030	.8784	0.0032
5	.8888	0.0036	.8987	0.0036	.9056	0.0034	.8634	0.0037
6	.8726	0.0042	.8838	0.0042	.8916	0.0040	.8442	0.0043
7	.7161	0.0100	0.0105	.7301	.7327	0.0106	.6623	0.0101
8	.7071	0.0105	0.0109	.7217	.7249	0.0110	.6522	0.0106
9	.6954	0.0111	0.0115	.7109	.7147	0.0116	.6393	0.0112
10	.9109	0.0031	0.0032	.9187	.9244	0.0030	.8924	0.0032
11	.8995	0.0036	0.0036	.9081	.9146	0.0034	.8789	0.0037
12	.8846	0.0042	0.0042	.8944	.9017	0.0040	.8615	0.0043

Palmetto Achievement Challenge Test of Mathematics

The South Carolina PACT of mathematics measures achievement of rigorous academic standards in grades three through eight. It is aligned with the state's mathematics curriculum (see South Carolina Department of Education, 1998a) that involves standards for Numbers and Operations, Algebra, Geometry, Measurement, and Data Analysis and Probability (see South Carolina Department of Education, 1998b). The test is also aligned with standards for the National Assessment of Educational Progress, National Council of Teachers of Mathematics, and Third International Mathematics and Science Standards. A purpose of the PACT was to increase academic performance of all students and, ultimately, raise high school graduation rates (Huynh et al., 2000). It was also used for accountability purposes and mandates

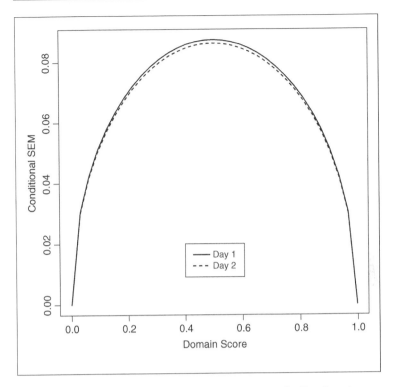

Figure 5.1. Conditional Standard Error of Measurement for Benchmark Assessment

established by the state and in The No Child Left Behind Act of 2001 (2002).

Achievement levels are demarked by three cut scores that were established through a bookmark standard setting procedure (see Cizek & Bunch, 2007). Individual scores and achievement levels are reported for examinees. PACT assessments involve four achievement levels: Below Basic, Basic, Proficient, and Advanced. Each level is defined by a performance level description that lists the knowledge and skills that examinees do and do not exhibit. For example, at the basic level a student can likely "find the mode by using either a stem-and-leaf plot or a group of numbers" (South Carolina Department of Education, 2005, p. 14), but the same student likely cannot "find the correct ordered pair for a point on the coordinate plane" (South Carolina Department of Education, 2005, p. 14).

Additional achievement-level descriptors further define performance at the Basic level but they are not listed here.

PACT mathematics assessments were administered on a single day in May. The 2006 sixth grade mathematics assessment contained 54 multiple-choice items scored 0 or 1, one constructed-response item scored from 0 to 2, and one constructed-response item scored from 0 to 4. Constructed-response items were scored by raters trained to score with an accuracy of 80% or higher. The reported score for a constructed-response item is the score assigned by the first rater. The highest possible raw score is 60.

Sample Results Section

The PACT sample consisted of 10,000 examinees randomly selected from a total of 52,673 students listed the grade six PACT mathematics data file. Male students were more prevalent (51%) than female students (49%). White (55%) and black (39%) students comprised the majority of the sample. Other race categories and students not reporting race represented about 6% of examinees. Across groups, average test performance varied by about 8 points (see Table 5.6) or about half of a standard deviation. Standard deviations ranged by about 1.7 points across groups.

A confirmatory factor analysis of tetrachoric and polychoric correlations supported the assumption if unidimensionality (details not shown). Error score correlations were not investigated. The only feature of the test design that may result in correlated errors was the use of raters to score the constructed response items.

Table 5.6
PACT Group Descriptive Statistics

Group	N	Mean	S.D.	KR-21
All	10,000	33.6269	11.3685	.9006
Male	5,149	33.0515	11.7609	.9078
Female	4,851	34.2377	10.9046	.8912
White	5,480	37.2124	10.8123	.8940
Black	3,900	28.7256	10.0772	.8670

This possibility was not explored, and caution is warranted when interpreting the results. The assumptions of essential τ-equivalence and congeneric scores were also not tested directly. Therefore, two reliability coefficients were reported for the PACT mathematics scores. Guttman's λ_2 and the Feldt-Gilmer coefficients were selected to address the assumptions of τ-equivalence and congeneric scores, respectively.

Reliability estimates listed in Table 5.7 for each type of coefficient are comparable. Indeed, the 95% confidence intervals suggest that results for the two coefficients are indistinguishable. Guttman's λ_2 estimates ranged from .8774 to .9146 across groups, and Feldt-Gilmer reliability estimates ranged from .8853 to .9153 across groups. The lowest estimates were observed for the black group.

Subkoviak and Huynh decision consistency indices are reported in Table 5.8. (Both methods are reported for illustration purposes.

Table 5.7
PACT Reliability Estimates, 95% Confidence Interval, and SEM

Group	Method	Value	95% Conf. Int. Lower	95% Conf. Int. Upper	SEM
All	Guttman's λ_2	.9083	.9061	.9105	3.4426
	Feldt-Gilmer	.9096	.9073	.9118	3.4181
Male	Guttman's λ_2	.9146	.9116	.9173	3.4369
	Feldt-Gilmer	.9159	.9131	.9186	3.4107
Female	Guttman's λ_2	.9010	.8974	.9045	3.4311
	Feldt-Gilmer	.9021	.8986	.9057	3.4119
White	Guttman's λ_2	.9032	.8999	.9065	3.3640
	Feldt-Gilmer	.9045	.9011	.9077	3.3413
Black	Guttman's λ_2	.8774	.8726	.8823	3.5825
	Feldt-Gilmer	.8790	.8739	.8838	3.5054

Note: Confidence intervals computed by the bootstrap percentile method with 1,000 bootstrap replications.

Table 5.8

PACT Decision Consistency Estimates and 95% Confidence Intervals

Group	Method	Value	95% Conf. Int. Lower	Upper
All	Subkoviak's Agreement	.7027	.6992	.7061
	Huynh's Agreement	.6960	.6940	.6980
	Huynh's κ	.5655	.5610	.5700
Male	Subkoviak's Agreement	.7128	.7079	.7179
	Huynh's Agreement	.7035	.7006	.7064
	Huynh's κ	.5790	.5729	.5851
Female	Subkoviak's Agreement	.6920	.6871	.6966
	Huynh's Agreement	.6878	.6851	.6905
	Huynh's κ	.5492	.5425	.5559
White	Subkoviak's Agreement	.6871	.6825	.6919
	Huynh's Agreement	.6835	.6806	.6864
	Huynh's κ	.5538	.5477	.5599
Black	Subkoviak's Agreement	.7210	.7158	.7265
	Huynh's Agreement	.7165	.7134	.7196
	Huynh's κ	.5460	.5391	.5529

Note: Confidence intervals for Subkoviak statistics computed by the bootstrap percentile method with 1,000 bootstrap replications.

In practice, only one method need be reported given the similarity of underlying assumptions.) Across all groups, percent agreement for the Huynh and Subkoviak methods was about 70%. Huynh's κ indicated about a 55% improvement over chance for all groups. The lowest decision consistency estimates were observed for the female group, and the highest were observed for the black group.

Conditional standard errors of measurement at each cut score are listed in Table 5.9. The largest amount of error occurs at the cut score between Below Basic and Basic. The standard error decreases

Table 5.9
PACT Conditional Standard Error of Measurement at the Cut
Scores

Group	Below Basic/Basic	Basic/Proficient	Proficient/ Advanced
All	3.8198	3.7190	3.2123
Male	3.8351	3.7339	3.2251
Female	3.7865	3.6865	3.1842
White	3.7855	3.6856	3.1834
Black	3.8110	3.7104	3.2048

as the cut score value increases. Conditional standard errors of measurement for the entire range of true scores are illustrated in Figure 5.2.

The Responsive Classroom Efficacy Study and MSCAN

The Responsive Classroom Efficacy Study is a randomized controlled trial conducted by a research team at the University of Virginia. The purpose of the study is to examine the impact of the Responsive Classroom Approach on student achievement and classroom quality. The study involves 24 schools randomized into either an intervention or control condition. Students are followed longitudinally from the spring of second grade to the spring of fifth grade. The study not only focuses on student achievement outcomes, but also attends to the mechanisms by which the Responsive Classroom Approach potentially affects student achievement. Thus, one of the primary aims of the study is to examine the extent to which the Responsive Classroom Approach impacts classroom quality, defined in terms of the interactions between teachers and children.

The research team initially began by relying exclusively on the CLASS measure (Pianta, La Paro, & Hamre, 2007) to assess quality, but soon learned that they needed an instrument to assess quality that took into consideration specific instructional techniques within mathematics education. They developed the

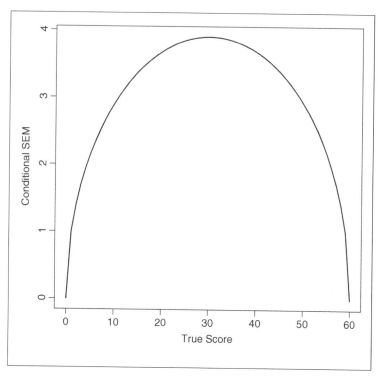

Figure 5.2. Conditional Standard Error of Measurement for PACT Mathematics

MSCAN as an adaptation of a set of constructs used by Borko, Stecher, and Kuffner (2007) in their SCOOP measure. Specifically, the MSCAN involves observation of a single elementary classroom mathematics lesson recorded on video tape. Raters grade the lesson on eight items, and each item is scored on a 1- to 7-point scale. Each lesson lasts between 45 and 75 minutes, but only 30 minutes are viewed for the ratings. Raters are experienced math educators who undergo a period of training before officially reporting scores.

A holistic scoring guide describes how features of the lesson translate into scores for each item. For example, the item Connectedness to Concepts receives a low score (e.g., 1 or 2) if the "Lesson uses elements of mathematics that can be memorized without requiring an understanding of the larger concepts." A high score is award to this item (e.g. 6 or 7) if

The lesson focuses on central concepts or "big ideas" and promotes generalization from specific instances to larger concepts or relationships. Students compare processes done with manipulatives to processes done in another method.

New raters are trained to use the scoring guide by experienced raters through participation in the rating process. However, new rater scores are not counted toward the final lesson score until they demonstrate proficiency with the scoring guide.

The MSCAN is currently in development, and the efficiency of the measurement procedure is in need of refinement. As it is currently implemented, items (I) and raters (R) represent two major sources of error for the MSCAN, and these facets are fully crossed with lesson (l). Specifically, data are collected through a $l \times R \times I$ design. This fully crossed design is time consuming. For example, it requires about 38 hours for three raters to score ten lessons. There are two ways to reduce the amount of time needed to score the MSAN. Reducing the number of raters is the easiest way to improve temporal efficiency. Using two raters to judge ten lessons would require about 25 hours, and this amount of work represents a reduction of 13 rating hours. The second way to improve efficiency is to use more raters and have each tape scored by a unique set of raters. This alternative design nests raters within lesson, $I \times (R : l)$. Ten tapes scored by three raters could be completed in about 13 hours with this design, but a tenfold increase in the number of raters would be needed. The additional cost of rater training may preclude the use of the $I \times (R : l)$ design, but a reliability estimate is needed to make an informed opinion.

Sample Results Section

A total of ten randomly selected lessons were observed independently by three raters. The average MSCAN score was 24.401, and the standard deviation was 7.6023. Demographics were not available at the time of the analysis, and the small sample size precluded a statistical test of unidimensionality. Therefore, caution is warranted when interpreting the results as they may differ by subgroup.

Lesson accounted for the largest portion of variance (33%), but only by a small margin (Table 5.10). Variance for the lesson by

Table 5.10
Generalizability Study Results for the MSCAN

Component	Variance (Standard Error)	Percent of Total
Lesson, *l*	0.7567	33
Items, *I*	0.2401	11
Raters, *R*	0.0155	1
Lesson × Items, *lI*	0.7141	32
Lesson × Raters, *lR*	0.1202	5
Raters × Items, *RI*	0.0104	0
Lesson × Raters × Items, *lRI*	0.4080	18
Total	2.2650	100

item interaction accounted for nearly as much variance (32%). This interaction suggests that error due to items is not consistent across lessons and the magnitude of this interaction is quite variable. Item error may be large for one lesson but small for another lesson. Rater and the rater-by-item interaction accounted for very little variance.

Table 5.11 lists the decision study results for four different data collection designs. The generalizability coefficient for the observed design was 0.838. Reducing the number of raters by one reduced

Table 5.11
Decision Study Results for the MSCAN

Design	Raters (n_r')	Generalizability Coefficient	SEM
$I \times R \times I$	3	0.8380	0.3825
	2	0.8123	0.4182
$I \times (R : I)$	3	0.8286	0.3956
	2	0.7992	0.4360

the generalizability coefficient to .8123. Each nested designs had a lower reliability than the corresponding (in terms of number of raters) crossed design.

Chapter Summary

Proper documentation of score reliability involves a large number of considerations that are detailed in the *Standards*. To facilitate the application of the *Standards*, a four-point outline was developed in this chapter. Documentation of score reliability should (a) characterize the examinee population and all major subpopulations, (b) describe the measurement procedure and all major sources of error, (c) present evidence in support of assumptions or discuss the consequences of unsupported assumptions, and (d) provide estimates of reliability and the standard error of measurement. Three example applications of the outline were then provided to demonstrate its applicability to a variety of measurement procedures.

Reliability documentation is only one part of a comprehensive technical document. Evidence of validity and test fairness should be included in a comprehensive document. For example, the proportion of items representing each part of a table of specifications would provide evidence of content validity, and a differential item functioning analysis would provide statistical evidence about test fairness. Even though reliability documentation was the focus of this chapter, comprehensive technical documentation should address validity, test fairness, and reliability. Becker and Pomplun (2006) describe an outline for information that should be included in a comprehensive technical document.

6

DISCUSSION AND
RECOMMENDED READINGS

A RELIABILITY ANALYSIS should be reported without judgment or evaluation. No statement should be made as to whether estimates of reliability estimate and standard error are good, acceptable, or bad. Estimates should speak for themselves, and a reader should be free to judge their value. Discussion of a reliability analysis should primarily focus on limitations of the analysis, such as unevaluated sources of error, untested assumptions, or weaknesses of the selected methods. Any additional discussion depends on the purpose of the analysis.

A reliability analysis conducted for an established measurement procedure or a test for which no changes are planned requires little else in the discussion. However, discussion of an analysis conducted for a measure in development should also include the recommended improvements and the empirical basis of the recommendations. For example, results from a decision study may be cited for recommending an increase (or reduction) in the number of raters judging a measurement procedure. The key to properly discussing recommendations is to use the analysis to provide empirical support for the recommended changes. For example, citing a generalizability coefficient that increases from .75 to .86 by adding an additional rater provides support for the recommendation of adding an additional rater. Citing the empirical basis for the recommendation adds credibility. A discussion section is an opportunity to make thoughtful recommendations for a measurement procedure in development. It is not a chance to capriciously modify a measurement procedure. Example discussion sections for the Benchmark assessment of English Language Arts (ELA), Palmetto Achievement Challenge Test (PACT) of mathematics, and the MSCAN are provided in the next three sections. Final comments and recommended readings conclude the chapter.

English Language Arts Benchmark Assessment

The complexity of the Benchmark data collection design necessitated the use of generalizability theory instead of classical test theory. Results indicate that an efficiency may be gained by reducing the total number of items from 64 to 56 (eliminate one item per testlet). This change lowers score reliability from .8015 to .791. Provided that the test specifications and test content are not affected, this change is recommended. However, the alternative data collection design should be pilot-tested prior to its operational use.

A limitation of the analysis is the lack of confidence intervals for the generalizability coefficients. However, the standard errors of the variance components suggested that the variance components were estimated precisely. Standard errors for the variance components were not listed in the results section, but the largest standard error was 0.0024 and the second largest was 0.0006.

Some Interesting Points About the Analysis

The Benchmark assessment of ELA was included as an example because it provides insight into a number of important aspects of reliability. One aspect was described in Chapter 2; splitting a test into two parts can be done in different ways, and each split can result in different underlying assumptions (e.g., parallel or congeneric). Another aspect is the importance of carefully considering the data collection design when choosing a method for estimating reliability (see Table 5. 3). A design that involves items and ignores occasion results in a larger reliability estimate. For example,

Cronbach's α is 0.9054 for the Benchmark assessment. This value is close to the estimate of 0.9159 for Design 10, which is a measure of internal consistency expressed in terms of generalizability theory. As Brennan (2001a) noted, measures of internal consistency can actually cause the reliability estimate to be an upper bound to reliability due to a hidden occasion facet. His observation is certainly true for the Benchmark Assessment. The estimate that includes an occasion facet (0.8015) is lower than the estimate that hides it (0.9159 and 0.9054). Obtaining the right estimate of reliability requires careful consideration of the data collection design. Ignoring important sources of error can lead to different conclusions about the consistency of test scores. Another aspect of the Benchmark analysis, or any analysis using generalizability theory, concerns the variability of variance components.

Reliability estimates obtained from data collection designs that differ from the observed design provide a suggestion of what reliability may be like for scores collected under the alternative design. Decision study results use variance components that are notorious for having large sampling variability. It is unlikely that results for one decision study will be exactly the same as results from another decision study (Gao & Brennan, 2001) using the same design. Consequently, the actual reliability estimate obtained from an alternative data collection design implemented as an observed design may not even be close to the suggested reliability estimate from a previous decision study. To the extent that sampling variability is the reason for a notable difference between the suggested and actual estimate and not a change in the population, greater confidence in the results from a decision study can be obtained by using a large sample size. However, the most cautious approach is to pilot an alternative data collection design as the observed design prior to implementing it as the operational design.

To understand this point more clearly, consider the results from the Benchmark assessment. Table 5.4 suggests that the generalizability coefficient will be .79 if Design 2 becomes the observed data collection design (i.e., becomes the operational design) upon the next administration of the measurement procedure. However, actual implementation of Design 2 may result in an estimate that is only in the ballpark of .79 due to (examinee) sampling variability. The actual estimate may be close to .79 or nowhere near it. The size of the ballpark really depends on the size of the examinee sample. Therefore, a conservative practice would pilot-test Design 2 as an observed design prior to making a whole-scale change to it. This practice would hopefully avoid the influence of chance on operational procedures.

Palmetto Achievement Challenge Test of Mathematics

A limitation of the PACT analysis was the exclusion of rater error and the treatment of constructed-response items. Two constructed-response items were scored by at least one rater. Operational costs and time constraints precluded the use of multiple raters for all examinees. A second rater scored constructed-response items for only 10% of the sample. Raters are an important source of error, but the influence of this source of error for the entire sample was not testable. As a result, the actual reliability may be lower than the reported values.

Subkoviak and Huynh decision consistency indices require binary items, but the PACT assessment included two constructed-response items. These items were included in the decision consistency analysis and computation of the conditional standard error of measurement by using the maximum possible score rather than the total number of items (see Huynh et al., 2000). This technique is reasonable given the small number of constructed-response items, but it is a possible limitation of the analysis.

The Responsive Classroom Efficacy Study and MSCAN

A fully crossed design with two raters or a nested design with three raters per lesson is a feasible alternative to the operational MSCAN design. Reliability for the observed MSCAN data collection design was about .84. Reducing the number of raters by one reduces reliability to .81; nesting raters within items results in a generalizability coefficient of about .83. Either alternative design is acceptable, but the nested design requires the additional cost of training more raters. If this cost is too high, then the fully crossed design with two raters is recommended. Given the small sample size, an alternative design should be pilot-tested before it is implemented operationally.

A limitation of the MSCAN analysis was the lack of demographic information. Reliability could not be examined for various groups. However, the small sample size might preclude such an analysis even if data were available on gender and race.

A second limitation was that dimensionality and error score correlations were not formally tested. The sample size was too small to conduct these tests. Caution is warranted, given that a violation of these assumptions may positively or negatively bias the reliability estimates.

A final limitation was the lack of confidence intervals for variance components. Standard errors were computed but not reported. The magnitudes of the standard errors (details not reported) suggest that the decision study results should be interpreted with caution. Variance components may notably differ from one administration to another with samples of only ten lessons. Therefore, the alternative designs should be pilot-tested before being used operationally.

Recommended Readings

There are several "must read" books on classical test theory. A good place to start is Gulliksen's *Theory of Mental Tests* (1950). This book is very readable but limited to parallel measures. It also predates some important developments, such as seminal work on strong true score theory. A more comprehensive and technical treatment is the classic *Statistical Theories of Mental Test Scores* by Lord and Novick (1968). This book is not only "the bible" on classical test theory but also a guide to modern test theories, such as item response theory. A more readable introduction to classical test theory is Traub's *Reliability for the Social Sciences: Theory and Applications* (1994). Recommended textbooks that cover classical test theory in addition to other topics are *Introduction to Measurement Theory* by Allen and Yen (1979) and *Introduction to Classical and Modern Test Theory* by Crocker and Algina (1986). Both of these texts include information on strong true score theory, but the latter also describes generalizability theory.

Cronbach and his colleagues published *The Dependability of Behavioral Measurement: Theory of Generalizability for Scores and Profiles* (1972) as a comprehensive guide for their work on the topic. Brennan's (2001b) text represents a more recent treatise on generalizability theory. Many recent developments and persisting challenges are also described in his book. A very readable introduction is Shavelson and Webb's *Generalizability Theory: A Primer* (1991). Their book is not only a good starting point for people interested in the subject but also a handy reference for designs commonly encountered in practice. Generalizability theory and other works on reliability are discussed in several comprehensive book chapters.

A chapter on reliability has been included in the book *Educational Measurement*, in all four editions. The chapter by Feldt and Brennan (1989) in the third edition and the chapter by Haertel (2006) in the fourth edition are thorough expositions on reliability. Each chapter describes reliability from the perspective of classical test theory, strong true score theory, and generalizability theory. Other topics, such as the reliability of difference scores, are also discussed. Each chapter represents the state of the art in its time.

Although textbooks provide context to work first presented in scholarly journals, reading original references has the benefit of seeing the author's own words and understanding their own thoughts. Journal articles are an unfiltered source of information on technical developments in the field. All of the references included in this textbook, as well as works cited in *Educational Measurement*, are highly recommended reads.

REFERENCES

The No Child Left Behind Act of 2001, Pub. L. No. 107–110 C.F.R. (2002).

Allen, M. J., & Yen, W. M. (1979). *Introduction to Measurement Theory*. Monterey, CA: Brooks/Cole.

Allen, N. L., Carlson, J. E., & Zelenak, C. A. (1999). *The NAEP 1996 Technical Report*. Washington D.C.: National Center for Education Statistics.

American Educational Research Association, American Psychological Association, & National Council on Measurement in Education. (1999). *Standards for educational and psychological testing*. Washington, D.C.: American Educational Research Association.

Angoff, W. H. (1953). Test reliability and effective test length. *Psychometrika, 18*, 1–14.

Becker, D. F., & Pomplun, M. R. (2006). Technical reporting and documentation. In S. M. Downing & T. M. Haladyna (Eds.), *Handbook of test development* (pp. 711–723). Mahwah, NJ: Lawrence Erlbaum Associates.

Bejar, I. I. (1991). *A generative approach to psychological and educational measurement*. Princeton, NJ: Educational Testing Service.

Bernardo, J. M. (1996). The concept of exchangeability and its applications. *Far East J. Math. Sci.*(Special Volume, Part II), 111–121.

Birnbaum, A. (1968). Some latent trait models and their use in inferring an examinee's ability. In F. M. Lord & M. R. Novick (Eds.), *Statistical theories of mental test scores*. Reading, MA: Addison-Wesley.

Borko, H., Stecher, B., & Kuffner, K. (2007). *Using artifacts to characterize reform-oriented instruction: The scoop notebook and rating guide*. Los Angeles: National Center for Research on Evaluation, Standards, and Student Testing (CRESST).

Brennan, R. L. (2001a). An essay on the history and future of reliability from the perspective of replications. *Journal of Educational Measurement, 38*(4), 295–317.

Brennan, R. L. (2001b). *Generalizability Theory.* New York: Springer-Verlag.

Brennan, R. L., & Kane, M. T. (1977). An index of dependability for mastery tests. *Journal of Educational Measurement, 14,* 277–289.

Brennan, R. L., & Wan, L. (2004). *A bootstrap procedure for estimating decision consistency for single-administration complex assessments.* Iowa City: Center for Advanced Studies in Measurement and Assessment.

Brown, W. (1910). Some experimental results in the correlation of mental abilities. *British Journal of Psychology,3,* 296–322.

Callender, J. C., & Osburn, H. G. (1979). An empirical comparison of coefficient alpha, Guttman's lambda – 2, and MSPLIT maximized split-half reliability estimates. *Journal of Educational Measurement, 16,* 89–99.

Cizek, G. J., & Bunch, M. B. (2007). *Standard setting: A guide to establishing and evaluating performance standards for tests.* Thousand Oaks CA: Sage.

Clopper, C. J., & Pearson, E. S. (1934). The use of confidence or fiducial limits illustrated in the case of the binomial. *Biometrika, 26,* 404–413.

Cohen, J. (1960). A Coefficient of Agreement for Nominal Scales.0020 *Educational and Psychological Measurement, 20*(1), 37–46.

Cortina, J. M. (1993). What is coefficient alpha? An examination of theory and applications. *Journal of Applied Psychology, 78*(1), 98–104.

Crocker, L., & Algina, J. (1986). *Introduction to classical and modern test theory.* New York: Holt, Rinehart, and Winston.

Cronbach, L. J. (1951). Coefficient alpha and the internal structure of tests. *Psychometrika, 16,* 297–334.

Cronbach, L. J., Gleser, G. C., Nanda, H., & Rajaratnam, N. (1972). *The dependability of behavioral measurements: Theory of generalizability for scores and profiles.* New York: John Wiley and Sons.

Cronbach, L. J., Rajaratnum, N., & Gleser, G. C. (1963). Theory of generalizability: A liberalization of reliability theory. *British Journal of Statistical Psychology, 16,* 137–163.

Cronbach, L. J., Schönemann, P., & McKie, D. (1965). Alpha coefficients for Stratified-Parallel Tests. *Educational and Psychological Measurement, 25*(2), 291–312.

Cronbach, L. J., & Shavelson, R. J. (2004). My current thoughts on coefficient alpha and successor procedures. *Educational and Psychological Measurement, 64,* 391–418.

Efron, B., & Tibshirani, R. J. (1993). *An introduction to the bootstrap.* Boca Raton, FL: Chapman & Hall/CRC.

Elliot, A. J., & McGregor, H. A. (2001). A 2 × 2 achievement goal framework. *Journal of Personality and Social Psychology, 80*(3), 501–519.

Fan, X., & Thompson, B. (2001). Confidence intervals about score reliability coefficients, please: An EPM guidelines editorial. *Educational and Psychological Measurement, 6*(4), 517–531.

Feldt, L. S. (1965). The approximate sampling distribution of Kuder-Richardson reliability coefficient 20. *Psychometrika, 30,* 357–370.

Feldt, L. S. (1975). Estimation of the reliability of a test divided into two parts of unequal length. *Psychometrika, 40*, 557–561.

Feldt, L. S. (2002). Estimating the internal consistency reliability of tests composed of testlets varying in length. *Applied Measurement in Education, 15*(1), 33–48.

Feldt, L. S., & Brennan, R. L. (1989). Reliability. In R. L. Linn (Ed.), *Educational Measurement* (3rd ed., pp. 105–146). New York: American Council on Education and MacMillan.

Feldt, L. S., & Qualls, A. L. (1996). Bias in coefficient alpha arising from heterogeneity. *Applied Measurement in Education, 9*(3), 277.

Feldt, L. S., Woodruff, D. J., & Salih, F. A. (1987). Statistical inference for coefficient alpha. *Applied Psychological Measurement, 11*, 93–103.

Finch, H., & Habing, B. (2007). Performance of DIMTEST- and NOHARM-Based Statistics for Testing Unidimensionality. *Applied Psychological Measurement, 31*(4), 292–307.

Gagné, P., & Hancock, G. R. (2006). Measurement Model Quality, Sample Size, and Solution Propriety in Confirmatory Factor Models. *Multivariate Behavioral Research, 41*(1), 65–83.

Gao, X., & Brennan, R. (2001). Variability of estimated variance components and related statistics in a performance assessment. *Applied Measurement in Education, 14*, 191–203.

Gilmer, J. S., & Feldt, L. S. (1983). Reliability estimation for a test with parts of unknown lengths. *Psychometrika, 48*, 99–111.

Glaser, R. (1963). Instructional technology and the measurement of learning outcomes. *American Psychologist, 18*, 519–521.

Green, S. B., & Hershberger, S. L. (2000). Correlated errors in true score models and their effect on coefficient alpha. *Structural Equation Modeling, 7*(2), 251–270.

Green, S. B., Lissitz, R. B., & Mulaik, S. A. (1977). Limitations of coefficient alpha as an index of test unidimensionality. *Educational and Psychological Measurement, 37*, 827–838.

Gulliksen, H. (1950). *Theory of mental tests*. Hillsdale, New Jersey: Lawrence Erlbaum.

Guttman, L. (1945). A basis for analyzing test-retest reliability. *Psychometrika, 10*(4), 255–282.

Haertel, E. H. (2006). Reliability. In R. L. Brennan (Ed.), *Educational Measurement* (4th ed., pp. 65–110). Westport, CT: American Council on Education and Praeger Publishers.

Hambleton, R. K., & Novick, M. R. (1973). Toward an integration of theory and method for criterion-referenced tests. *Journal of Educational Measurement, 10*(3), 159–170.

Hanson, B. A., & Brennan, R. L. (1990). An investigation of classification consistency indexes estimated under alternative strong true score models. *Journal of Educational Measurement, 27*(4), 345–359.

Hogg, R. V., & Tanis, E. A. (2001). *Probability and statistical inference* (6th ed.). Upper Saddle River, NJ: Prentice Hall.

Huynh, H. (1976a). On the reliability of decisions in domain-referenced testing. *Journal of Educational Measurement, 13*(4), 253–264.

Huynh, H. (1976b). Statistical consideration of mastery scores. *Psychometrika, 41*(1), 65–78.

Huynh, H., Meyer, J. P., & Barton, K. (2000). *Technical documentation for the 1999 Palmetto Achievement Challenge Tests of English language arts and mathematics, grade three through eight.* Columbia, SC: South Carolina Department of Education.

Johnson, R. L., Penny, J. A., & Gordon, B. (2009). *Assessing performance: Designing, scoring, and validating performance tasks.* New York: Guilford Press.

Jöreskog, K. G. (1971). Statistical analysis of sets of congeneric tests. *Psychometrika, 36*(2), 109–133.

Kane, M. T. (2002). Inferences about variance components and reliability-generalizability coefficients in the absence of random sampling. *Journal of Educational Measurement, 39*, 165–181.

Kane, M. T. (2006). Validation. In R. L. Brennan (Ed.), *Educational Measurement* (4th ed., pp. 17–64). Westport, CT: American Council on Education and Praeger Publishers.

Keats, J. A. (1957). Estimation of error variance of test scores. *Psychometrika, 22*(1), 29–41.

Keats, J. A., & Lord, F. M. (1962). A theoretical distribution for mental test scores. *Psychometrika, 27*(1), 59–72.

Kelley, T. L. (1947). *Fundamentals of statistics.* Cambridge, MA: Harvard University Press.

Keppel, G., & Wickens, T. D. (2004). *Design and analysis: A researcher's handbook.* Upper Saddle River, NJ: Pearson Prentice Hall.

Kline, R. B. (1998). *Principles and practice of structural equation modeling.* New York: Guilford.

Kolen, M., J. (2006). Scaling and norming. In R. L. Brennan (Ed.), *Educational Measurement* (4th ed., pp. 155–186). Westport, CT: American Council on Education and Praeger Publishers.

Komaroff, E. (1997). Effect of simultaneous violations of essential τ-equivalence and uncorrelated error on coefficient α. *Applied Psychological Measurement, 21*, 337–348.

Kopriva, R. J., & Shaw, D. G. (1991). Power estimates: The effect of dependent variable reliability on the power of one-factor ANOVAs. *Educational and Psychological Measurement, 51*, 585–595.

Kristof, W. (1974). Estimation of reliability and true score variance from a split of a test into three arbitrary parts. *Psychometrika, 39*, 491–499.

Kuder, G. F., & Richardson, M. W. (1937). Theory and estimation of test reliability. *Psychometrika, 2*(3), 151–160.

Lee, W.-C. (2007). Multinomial and compound multinomial error models for tests with complex item scoring. *Applied Psychological Measurement, 31*, 255–274.

Linn, R. L., & Gronlund, N. E. (2000). *Measurement and assessment in teaching* (8th ed.). Upper Saddle River, NJ: Prentice-Hall.

Livingston, S. A. (1972). Criterion-referenced applications of classical test theory. *Journal of Educational Measurement, 9*(1), 13–26.

Lord, F. M. (1955a). Estimating test reliability. *Educational and Psychological Measurement, 15,* 325–336.

Lord, F. M. (1955b). Sampling fluctuations resulting from the sampling of test items. *Psychometrika, 20*(1), 1–22.

Lord, F. M. (1965). A strong true-score theory, with applications. *Psychometrika, 30*(3), 239–270.

Lord, F. M., & Novick, M. R. (1968). *Statistical theories of mental test scores.* Reading, MA: Addison-Wesley.

Lucke, J. F. (2005). "Rassling the Hog": The influence of correlated error on internal consistency, classical reliability, and congeneric reliability. *Applied Psychological Measurement, 29,* 106–125.

Osburn, H. G. (2000). Coefficient alpha and related internal consistency reliability coefficients. *Psychological Methods, 5*(3), 343–355.

Pianta, R. C., La Paro, K., & Hamre, B. (2007). *Classroom assessment scoring system [CLASS] Manual, K-3.* Baltimore, MD: Paul H. Brookes Publishing Company.

Popham, W. J., & Husek, T. R. (1969). Implications of criterion-referenced measurement. *Journal of Educational Measurement, 6*(1), 1–9.

Qualls, A. L. (1995). Estimating the reliability of a test containing multiple item formats. *Applied Measurement in Education, 8*(2), 111–120.

Qualls, A. L., & Moss, A. D. (1996). The degree of congruence between test standards and test documentation within journal publications. *Educational and Psychological Measurement, 56,* 209–214.

Rajaratnam, N., Cronbach, L. J., & Gleser, G. C. (1965). Generalizability of stratified-parallel tests. *Psychometrika, 30,* 39–56.

Raju, N. S. (1970). New formula for estimating total test reliability from parts of unequal length. *Proceedings of the 78th Annual Convention of the American Psychological Association, 5,* 143–144.

Raju, N. S. (1977). A generalization of coefficient alpha. *Psychometrika, 42*(4), 549–565.

Raykov, T. (1997). Estimation of composite reliability for congeneric measures. *Applied Psychological Measurement, 21,* 173–184.

Raykov, T. (1998). Coefficient Alpha and Composite Reliability With Interrelated Nonhomogeneous Items. *Applied Psychological Measurement, 22*(4), 375–385.

Raykov, T. (2001). Bias of coefficient α for fixed congeneric measures with correlated errors. *Applied Psychological Measurement, 25,* 69–76.

Ree, M. J., & Carretta, T. R. (2006). The role of measurement error in familiar statistics. *Organizational Research Methods, 9,* 99–112.

Reuterberg, S.-E., & Gustafsson, J.-E. (1992). Confirmatory factor analysis and reliability: Testing measurement model assumptions. *Educational and Psychological Measurement, 52,* 795–811.

Rost, J. (1990). Rasch models in latent classes: An integration of two approaches to item analysis. *Applied Psychological Measurement, 14,* 271–282.

Rulon, P. J. (1939). A simplified procedure for determining the reliability of a test by split-halves. *Harvard Educational Review, 9,* 99–103.

Schmitt, N. (1996). Uses and abuses of coefficient alpha. *Psychological Assessment, 8,* 350–353.

Shavelson, R. J., & Webb, N. (1991). *Generalizability Theory: A primer.* Thousand Oaks, CA: Sage.

South Carolina Department of Education. (1998a). *Mathematics: South Carolina curriculum standards.* Columbia, SC: South Carolina Department of Education.

South Carolina Department of Education. (1998b). *PACT mathematics assessment: A blueprint for success.* Columbia, SC: South Carolina Department of Education.

South Carolina Department of Education. (2002). English language arts curriculum standards 2002. Retrieved January 30, 2007, from http://ed.sc. gov/agency/offices/cso/standards/ela

South Carolina Department of Education. (2005). *Performance-Level descriptors for the Palmetto Achievement Challenge Tests.* Columbia, SC: South Carolina Department of Education.

Spearman, C. (1904). The proof and measurement of association between two things. *American Journal of Psychology, 15,* 72–101.

Spearman, C. (1910). Correlation calculated from faulty data. *British Journal of Psychology, 3,* 271–295.

Stevens, J. (1996). *Applied multivariate statistics for the social sciences* (3rd. ed.). Mahwah, NJ: Lawrence Erlbaum Associates.

Stout, W. (1987). A nonparametric approach for assessing latent trait unidimensionality. *Psychometrika, 52,* 589–617.

Subkoviak, M. J. (1976). Estimating reliability from a single administration of a criterion-referenced test. *Journal of Educational Measurement, 13*(4), 265–276.

Subkoviak, M. J. (1978). Empirical investigation of procedures for estimating reliability for mastery tests. *Journal of Educational Measurement, 15*(2), 111–116.

Swaminathan, H., Hambleton, R. K., & Algina, J. J. (1975). A Bayesian decision-theoretic procedure for use with criterion-referenced tests. *Journal of Educational Measurement, 12*(2), 87–98.

Thompson, B., & Vacha-Haase, T. (2000). Psychometrics is datametrics: The test is not reliable. *Educational and Psychological Measurement, 60,* 174–195.

Traub, R. E. (1994). *Reliability for the social sciences: Theory and applications.* Thousand Oaks, CA: Sage.

Traub, R. E., & Rowley, G. L. (1991). An NCME instructional module on Understanding Reliability. *Educational Measurement: Issues and Practice, 10*(1), 171–179.

Vacha-Haase, T., Kogan, L. R., & Thompson, B. (2000). Sample compositions and variabilities in published studies versus those in test manuals: validity of score reliability inductions. *Educational and Psychological Measurement, 60,* 509–522.

van der Linden, W., & Glass, C. A. W. (Eds.). (2000). *Computerized adaptive testing: Theory and practice.* Dordrecht, The Netherlands: Kluwer Academic Publishers.

Wainer, H., Bradlow, E. T., & Wang, X. (Eds.). (2007). *Testlet Response Theory and Its Applications.* New York: Cambridge University Press.

Wainer, H., & Kiely, G. L. (1987). Item clusters and computerized adaptive testing: A case for testlets. *Journal of Educational Measurement, 24,* 185–201.

Waller, N. G. (2008). Comingled samples: A neglected source of bias in reliability analysis. *Applied Psychological Measurement, 32*, 211–223.

Whittington, D. (1998). How well do researchers report their measures?: An evaluation of measurement in published educational research. *Educational and Psychological Measurement, 58*, 21–37.

Zimmerman, D. W., & Williams, r. H. (1980). Is classical test theory 'robust' under violation of the assumption of uncorrelated errors? *Canadian journal of Psychology, 34*, 227–237.

Zimmerman, D. W., Zumbo, B. D., & LaLonde, C. (1993). Coefficient alpha as an estimate of test reliability under violation of two assumptions. *Educational and Psychological Measurement, 53*, 33–49.

INDEX

Made in the USA
San Bernardino, CA
11 January 2018